Why I W

While teaching this unique seminar two requests have persistently surfaced. Students who have taken the seminar have asked if there is a book that gives all the details of each lesson so that the material may be reviewed or shared with a friend. Others have expressed a deep desire to teach the seminar in the future, and have asked if there is a teachers' manual that would aid them in preparation.

This book is an attempt to provide the needed help to both these groups, with just a single volume. If you are in the student group, you will benefit by reading the material as a regular book. You will not need a lesson guide and you do not need to be concerned about the changes in the type. If you are using this book as a preparation for teaching this seminar, it will be helpful to have a blank lesson in front of you to compare.

1. **The questions listed in each lesson are in bold type.**
2. *The scripture texts are in bold italic type.*
3. <u>**THE ANSWERS ARE IN UNDERLINED CAPS.**</u>
4. The notes found in the lessons, along with personal comments I make, are given in small, regular type, as does the lesson guides.
5. The answers to all the quizzes are in the back of the book.

"Blessed is he who reads (the teacher) and those who hear (the students) of this prophecy." Revelation 1:3

Harry Robinson

Cover Design by Sarah Symington
The Hamblin Company

To order additional copies of this book:
Call (828) 699-3447

Copyright © 2015 by Harry Robinson Revelation Seminars,
All Rights Reserved
Printed in the United States of America

Unless otherwise noted, all texts quoted in this book are from the
New King James Version® of the Bible. Copyright © 1982 by Thomas Nelson.
Used by permission. All rights reserved.

ISBN 978-0-9742729-5-5

A JOURNEY INTO THE FUTURE

Making Sense
of the Book
of Revelation

Harry Robinson
2014

A Journey into the Future
Lesson No. 1

What Is This Book?

This book of the Bible that we are about to study is very unique among the books of Scripture. Its uniqueness stems from the nature of the information found in it, being mainly about the future. When Moses wrote the book of Genesis, he dealt with events that were all in his past. When the gospel writers wrote their accounts of the life and teachings of Jesus, their material also dealt with what had already taken place. While the information which John recorded in this last book of the Bible briefly refers to some events in John's past, the overwhelming amount of information focuses on events in John's future --- and even in ours.

1. Who is giving this information?

    "The Revelation of Jesus Christ, which God gave Him to show His servants --- things which must shortly take place. And He sent and signified it by His angel to His servant John." Revelation 1:1.

It is **JESUS CHRIST** Himself! This information is not coming from John --- he is just passing it on to us. This is a special book from Jesus. No other book of the Bible is described as coming directly from Him. Since Jesus is so special to us, this particular book holds a great deal of interest for us.

In the phrase, "Revelation of Jesus Christ," the preposition "of" can have two different meanings. It could mean the revelation is *from* Jesus, or that the revelation is *about* Jesus. Verse 1 itself chooses for us the correct meaning.

What is it that is revealed in this book?

It clearly states that it will reveal to us **THINGS WHICH MUST SHORTLY TAKE PLACE**. The main focus of this book is events, not theology, although theological concepts are very much a part of it. Its central theme is to acquaint us with some special events that are to happen on earth. While we shall surely learn a lot about Jesus Himself in this book, it is not a biography of Jesus, as are the four gospels. Rather, it is a book that is focused on special events to take place in the future.

When?

Since we now know that this book is all about events, the question naturally arises, when can we expect these things to occur?

2.   **When was John told these things would happen?**

> *"Then he said to me, 'These words are faithful and true.' And the Lord God of the holy prophets sent His angel to show His servants the things which must shortly take place." Revelation 22:6.*

SHORTLY. Here the same word is used as in verse 1 of Chapter 1. It is easy to come to a quick conclusion that these Revelation events would occur very soon after the information was given to John in vision. However, notice verse 7.

3.   **What would happen soon after these things?**

> *"Behold, I am coming quickly! Blessed is he who keeps the words of the prophecy of this book." Revelation 22:7.*

This is **JESUS' SECOND COMING**. It occurs quickly after the Revelation events, and this means that the Revelation events happen "shortly" before that great event, not shortly after John's day.
There is little doubt in the minds of most Bible students that Revelation focuses strongly upon events that will take place just a short while before the arrival of Jesus Christ to our planet for the second time. This event is referred to as the second coming, or the second advent of Christ.

That short period of time just prior to Christ's return is spoken of by Bible writers as the "last days," and refers to the short span of time just before the end of the world.

Although this time period is relatively short, it is packed full of enormously important events. The book of Revelation is one of the main textbooks used to study this special era of earth's history.

Revelation's Three Time Periods

We will meet several time periods in the book of Revelation, but it is very helpful for students to step back from the trees to get a bird's eye view of the forest of time periods upon which Revelation is focused. All time periods we will encounter in the book are included in these three distinct eras of time, which can be diagramed as follows:

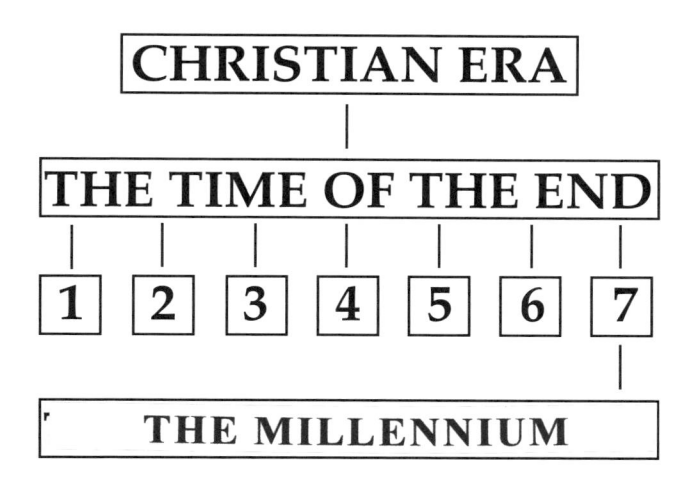

```
              CHRISTIAN ERA
                    |
          THE TIME OF THE END
         |  |  |  |  |  |  |
         1  2  3  4  5  6  7
                           |
              THE MILLENNIUM
```

The Christian Era stretches from John's day down to our day. It is the longest time period of the three --- about 2,000 years in length.

The time of the end is a short, but intense period of time shortly before the arrival of Christ back to planet earth. It is the main period of time engrossing the attention of Revelation, and its major events will be delineated as seven in number, as will become apparent in our study.

The Millennium, the final time period, is 1,000 years in length. While it is technically the seventh part of the Time of the End events, it is treated by Revelation as a distinct, separate time period, for a reason we will eventually discover in our studies.

Chapters	*Time Period Involved*
1-3	THE CHRISTIAN ERA
4-19	THE TIME OF THE END
20-22	THE MILLENNIUM

The first three chapters of Revelation focus on the first time period, and the last three chapters focus on the third time period. The overwhelming portion of Revelation (16 of the 22 chapters) are concerned with this unique time period that will produce events of momentous import, Bible students call "The Time of the End." The events predicted are of immense interest to us, as we now stand on the threshold of that time.

Revelation's Target Audience

4.   **Who were the first readers of this book?**

"I, Jesus, have sent My angel to testify to you these things in the churches. I am the Root and the Offspring of David, the Bright and the Morning Star." Revelation 22:16.

Notice that Jesus had a specific group in mind for which the book was written. He had in mind **CHURCH MEMBERS**.

The information in this book was primarily for believers, not unbelievers. The reason for this was that believers had a basic knowledge of the Scriptures, and this background knowledge is an indispensible key to understanding the book of Revelation.

We know this is true from the prolific use of those Scriptures by the book of Revelation. The book borrows so much of its contents from other scriptures, that almost nothing in it is original with Revelation itself. Of the 404 verses in the book, 276 of them contain material found elsewhere in the Bible. This means that Revelation is significantly linked to other books of the Bible --- a fact that will be an eye-opener to us as we progress in our study.

The All-Important Key

5.   **What did Jesus use to give a Bible study?**

"Then He said to them, 'O foolish ones, and slow of heart to believe in all that the prophets have spoken! Ought not the Christ to have suffered these things and to enter into His glory?' And beginning at Moses and all the Prophets, He expounded to them in all the Scriptures the things concerning Himself." Luke 24:25-27.

Jesus did not mention just one single Scripture; He utilized **ALL THE SCRIPTURES**. Jesus' method of teaching in Revelation is identical to the method He used in His earthly ministry. It's the bed-rock principle of interpreting the book of Revelation and also the way we study other parts of the Bible. What it means is that we "let the Bible explain itself." This method of study is clearly encouraged in the Bible.

6.   **What method did the apostle Paul use to teach?**

> *"These things we also speak, not in words which man's wisdom teaches but which the Holy Spirit teaches, comparing spiritual things with spiritual."* *I Corinthians 2:13.*

Paul advocated utilizing **COMPARISON** in our use of the Scriptures. It is not safe to make any conclusions about what we read in the Bible without first checking with supportive material from other Bible books. Doing this will prevent us from misunderstanding the Word of God.

Sometime ago, while driving home from an errand, I pulled up behind a small delivery van that was waiting for the red light to change. Immediately I noticed a prominent sign on the back of the vehicle. It said, "CAUTION, BLIND DRIVER." As you might guess, this immediately caught my attention, and my mind whirled with exciting thoughts. I thought, "Wow, how marvelous is modern technology!" I had heard of many types of devices that allowed physically disabled people to enjoy the freedom of driving, but apparently, they could even assist a blind person to drive! I could hardly wait to get home and announce to my wife, "Now even blind people can drive a vehicle!"

Being sure that I would be challenged about that conclusion, I decided to follow the van. When the driver stopped for the next red light, I pulled up beside him to get a look at him with my own eyes.

As I slowly pulled along side of this marvelous vehicle, I then noticed another sign, this one on the side of the van. It said, "CAROLINA WINDOW AND BLIND COMPANY." I suddenly saw another meaning to the sign that I first saw on the back of the van. How relieved I was for this additional information!

How much misunderstanding of the Bible has resulted from people taking one verse of Scripture and arguing with vehemence about what they insist the Bible teaches. If they had bothered to check out other passages of the Bible that dealt with the same concept, it would avoid a plethora of argument and misunderstanding. In other words, let us allow the Bible to explain itself.

7.   **How much of the Bible is useful to us?**

"All Scripture is given by inspiration of God, and is profitable for doctrine, for reproof, for correction, for instruction in righteousness, that the man of God may be complete, thoroughly equipped for every good work." II Timothy 3:16, 17.

In our study of the book of Revelation, we will not restrict ourselves to it, superimposing our personal ideas and theories on what we find there. Instead we will allow **ALL SCRIPTURE** to be a resource for us.

No part of Scripture is an island unto itself, unrelated to other parts of God's Word. There is a beautiful harmony throughout. What we do not understand in one place can be made clear to us by checking in other places that speak of the same or similar ideas. In no part of Scripture is that more true than with the book of Revelation.

Therefore, we will lean heavily upon this method in our course of study. Following this method of interpretation will not only help us understand Revelation, but we will also come away with a better understanding of all the Scriptures, "which are able to make thee wise unto salvation." II Timothy 3:15.

Revelation's Bridge to Somewhere
Lesson No. 2

Bridges

Bridges are indispensible to man. They enable us to get from one vantage point to another, spanning otherwise impossible barriers, such as rivers, canyons, or busy freeways.

Jesus has built a bridge to get us from John's day to that special time called the time of the end. That bridge is described in the first three chapters of Revelation. It is not a bridge of steel or stone, but is built with prophetic predictions.

A Prophetic Bridge

1. What event does John first mention in his book?

   "Behold, He is coming with clouds, and every eye will see Him, even they who pierced Him. And all the tribes of the earth will mourn because of Him. Even so, Amen." Revelation 1:7.

It is **JESUS' SECOND COMING**, rather than His first coming, that is uppermost in the mind of the writer. The major focus of this book is the second coming of Christ to earth. The short period of time just before He returns is referred to as "the last days," or "the time of the end." This brief period of time is packed full of enormously important events, referred to as "things which must shortly take place" (verse 1).

It is essential to know when this special period of time has arrived, but John was not given any specific date. Instead, he was given the first vision of Revelation, a seven-fold prophecy, that would act like a "bridge," taking us from a known point (John's day) to an unknown point (the time of the end).

Jesus could easily have indicated to John a specific future date, or a time prophecy that would reveal to John the exact amount of time between his day and the time of the end. It was not necessary for John to know this, since the time of the end was far removed from his day. Nor would it have been helpful for those living during that interim of time to be told that the end of all things was far beyond their lifetime. Jesus said to His disciples, "Therefore you also be ready, for the Son of Man is coming at an hour you do not expect." Matthew 24:44.

Yet, it would be important for those living just before that time of the end, or those living through it, to realize the seriousness of the times. Therefore, Jesus created this prophecy in such a way as to hide the exact time from the understanding of those living at the beginning or during the long interim, yet could be easily discerned by those living at the end of it. We are there now --- at the end of this prophetic bridge, and the time of the end is upon us. Jesus invented this marvelous "bridge prophecy" and, as we study it we will sense that "the end of all things is at hand." I Peter 4:7.

2. **What seven things make up this prophecy?**

> *"I was in the Spirit on the Lord's Day, and I heard behind me a loud voice, as of a trumpet, saying, 'I am the Alpha and the Omega, the First and the Last,' and, 'What you see, write in a book and send it to the seven churches which are in Asia, to Ephesus, to Smyrna, to Pergamos, to Thyatira, to Sardis, to Philadelphia, and to Laodicea.' " Revelation 1:10, 11.*

This prophetic outline has **SEVEN CHURCHES** to it. Each segment was a local church in John's day. There were many more churches in the area, but these were chosen for the peculiar experience they were going through. They were also chosen for their location. If one traveled over the main Roman highway through Asia Minor, he would come to each of these cities in the order listed.

Seven Churches of Asia Minor

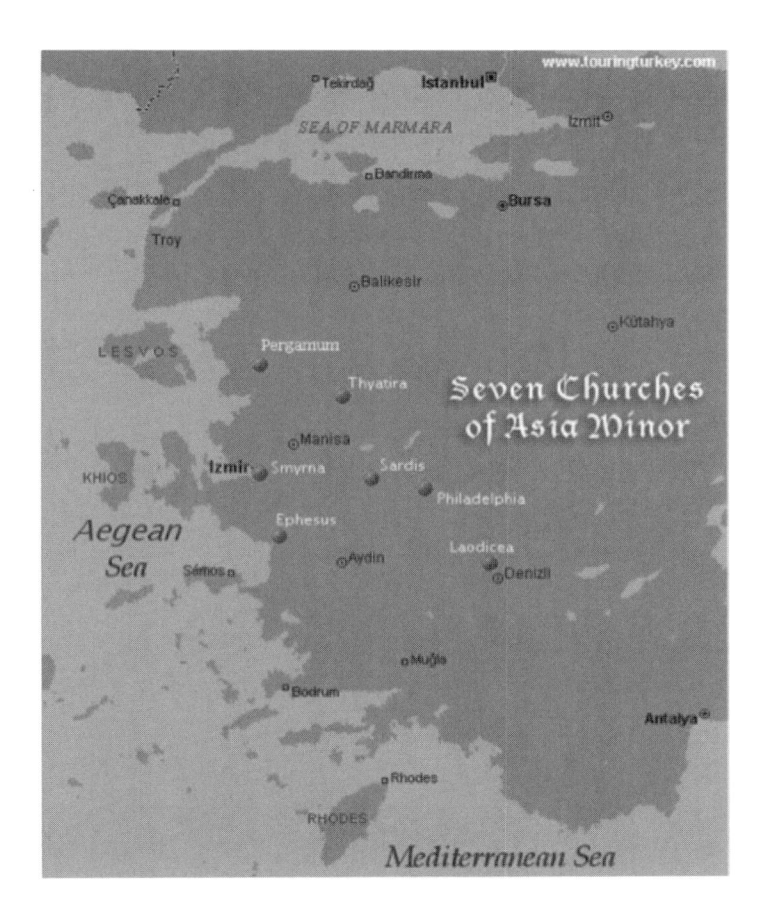

3. **What two things are represented by what John saw in these seven churches?**

"Write the things which you have seen, and the things which are, and the things which will take place after this." Revelation 1:19.

Jesus is here speaking to John in the Greek language. He uses the word "and" twice. In Greek this word has two different meanings, and the context dictates which meaning to choose. The Greek word for "and" can be used to connect two different things together, and is called a "copulative and". A second use is to further explain what has already been said, and is called an "explanatory and." Verse 19 does not make logical sense if you assume both "ands" are copulative, or both "ands" are explanatory. The only sensible way to understand what Jesus is saying is to see that He used the first "and" as explanatory, and the second "and" to couple two different things. Modern translations, such as the New Living Translation, make this clear: "Write down what you have seen --- both the things that are now happening and the things that will happen later." So the things John now sees are **[1] THINGS WHICH ARE, and [2] THINGS WHICH WILL TAKE PLACE AFTER THIS**.

These individual messages do not describe political events, but spiritual experiences the people of God would go through during the centuries spanning the Christian era, from John's time to the time of the end. What is even more interesting is the fact that in the centuries to follow, those seven different experiences happened to the Christian church in the very order in which they are listed in Revelation. This can easily be recognized from a look at history.

Keep clearly in your mind that the things of this prophecy are not the things that will happen during the time of the end. Those things will be shown to John in his next vision. The things of this prophecy will begin immediately, with John's time, and will lead us up to the events of the time of the end that will be revealed to John in his next vision. In other words, the events of this prophecy are not the events of the time of the end. They all happen before the prophetic events of the time of the end, which also are seven in number.

We will now look briefly at the experience of each of these local churches and show how they accurately mirror the experience of general Christendom. Since the first church starts in John's day ("things which are"), it is easy to assume that Jesus has in mind a representation of the apostolic church (the years that the apostles were alive).

[1] EPHESUS > FAITHFUL
31-100 A.D.

4.   What kind of people did they not accept?

> *"To the angel of the church of Ephesus write, These things says He who holds the seven stars in His right hand, who walks in the midst of the seven golden lampstands: 'I know your works, your labor, your patience, and that you cannot bear those who are evil. And you have tested those who say they are apostles and are not, and have found them liars; and you have persevered and have patience, and have labored for My name's sake and have not become weary. Nevertheless I have this against you, that you have left your first love. Remember therefore from where you have fallen; repent and do the first works, or else I will come*

to you quickly and remove your lampstand from its place --- unless you repent. But this you have, that you hate the deeds of the Nicolaitans, which I also hate.'"
Revelation 2:1-6.

There are three kinds of people mentioned here. In verse 2 they are singled out as **[1] EVIL** and **[2] LIARS**. In verse 6 a special group, called **[3] NICOLAITANS** is added to the list. This last group may not be familiar to you. The Nicolaitans were a group who maintained that the deeds the body committed did not affect the soul and, therefore, had no bearing on salvation. They were the forerunners of those who claim to love Jesus while they deliberately ignore, or disobey, what He asks of us. We can read clear warnings against such deadly heresy in I John 2:3-6 and James 2:14-20.

While the apostles were still alive, Christians experienced some troublesome times, but soon after the apostles died, Christianity plunged into a time of serious persecutions, and that is pictured by the experience of the second church.

[2] SMYRNA > TRIBULATION
100-313 A.D.

5.   What type of experience did this church have?

"And to the angel of the church in Smyrna write, These things says the First and the Last, who was dead, and came to life: I know your works, tribulation, and poverty (but you are rich); and I know the blasphemy of those who say they are Jews and are not, but are a synagogue of Satan. Do not fear any of those things which you are about to suffer. Indeed, the devil is about to throw some of you into prison, that you may be tested, and you will have tribulation ten days. Be faithful until death, and I will give you the crown of life." Revelation 2:8-10.

For about 200 years Christians experienced an immense amount of **TRIBULATION**. This persecution was done by the Roman Empire, which considered Christianity illegal and a threat to the pagan religion the government fostered. The turning point came with the nominal conversion to Christianity of Constantine, a Roman Emperor. He opened the rich treasury of the Roman Empire to Christianity, building huge and expensive cathedrals for the people, even paying the Christian leaders and pastors.

All this financial support came with strings attached. When Christians were pressured by the pagan government to change many of their beliefs to accommodate some pagan beliefs, Christians found it expedient to compromise their biblical faith and "adapt" their religion to that of their pagan benefactors. This brought about some significant changes in Christian belief and practices, as represented by the third church.

[3] PERGAMOS> COMPROMISE
313-538 A.D.

6. Who were now accepted by the church?

> *"And to the angel of the church in Pergamos write, These things says He who has the sharp two-edged sword: I know your works, and where you dwell, where Satan's throne is. And you hold fast to My name, and did not deny My faith even in the days in which Antipas was My faithful martyr, who was killed among you, where Satan dwells. But I have a few things against you, because you have there those who hold the doctrine of Balaam, who taught Balak to put a stumbling block before the children of Israel, to eat things sacrificed to idols, and commit sexual immorality. Thus you also have those who hold the doctrine of the Nicolaitans, which thing I hate." Revelation 2:12-15.*

This is the second time the **NICOLAITANS** are singled out by Christ. The first church, Ephesus, would not allow them to be part of their fellowship, but at this time we find them actually accepted into the church! This is an indication of the compromising that was going on among Christians. During these centuries numerous pagan beliefs and practices were introduced, which distorted and even cancelled out some vital Bible truths. Many of these unbiblical ideas are still strongly held by some today, who are unaware of the origin of these strange ideas.

Compromising our beliefs never leads upward to better spirituality, but always heads downward to eventual total apostasy, and that is the testimony of the history of Christianity.

[4] THYATIRA > APOSTASY
538-1500 A.D.

7. What Bible character is used to represent church leadership which promoted this outright disobedience to God?

> *"And to the angel of the church in Thyatira write, These things says the Son of God, who has eyes like a flame of fire, and His feet like fine brass: I know your works, love, service, faith, and your patience; and as for your works, the last are more than the first. Nevertheless I have a few things against you, because you allow that woman Jezebel, who calls herself a prophetess, to teach and seduce My servants to commit sexual immorality and eat things sacrificed to idols. Revelation 2:18-20.*

JEZEBEL was a heathen woman in the Old Testament who Ahab, the king of Israel, married. She was a very strong, aggressive woman, and used her position of influence to amalgamate the Jewish religion with her pagan beliefs. The people got so far away from God that God sent a special prophet named Elijah to confront the situation and bring people back to keeping the commandments of God.

The Jezebel-led apostasy of Old Testament times fitly represents the long period of Christianity's apostasy of over 1,000 years. This period is often referred to as the Dark Ages. Just as Elijah brought the people back to the truths of God's Word, so the Reformation movement toward the end of the Dark Ages brought the light of truth to many, causing sweeping changes in the way people related to God's Word.

This is why Jesus said about this era of time, "and as for your works, the last are more than the first" (verse 19). One would think that things would do nothing but improve, but the experience of the next church pictures the opposite.

[5] SARDIS > BACKSLIDING
1500-1800 A.D.

8. **How is their spirituality described in verse 1?**

> *"And to the angel of the church in Sardis write, These things says He who has the seven Spirits of God and the seven stars: I know your works, that you have a name that you are alive, but you are dead." Revelation 3:1.*

They have a name (reputation) that they are spiritually **ALIVE**, but their true spiritual state, according to Jesus who sees all things, is that they are **DEAD**. The Reformation was a "protest" against unbiblical traditions and abuses promoted by the church leaders of the times. Great strides were made in acquainting the common people with what the Bible actually taught. Strong, spiritual denominations, still existing today, were established by Bible-centered preachers. Sadly, when these founding fathers passed away, their followers ceased to grow spiritually and even regressed to many unbiblical beliefs from the past.

In spite of this regrettable situation, the next church experiences a radical change for the better.

[6] PHILADELPHIA> BACK TO THE BIBLE
1800s

9.   How do these people respond to God's Word?

> *"And to the angel of the church in Philadelphia write, These things says He who is holy, He who is true, He who has the key of David, He who opens and no one shuts, and shuts and no one opens. I know your works. See, I have set before you an open door, and no one can shut it, for you have a little strength, have kept My word, and have not denied My name,"* Revelation 3:7, 8.

Jesus commends them because they **KEPT GOD'S WORD**. These are clearly Bible-centered believers. During this time, great revivals broke out across Christendom, sparked by a close study of the Bible. Also, it was during this time the British and American Bible Societies came into existence, encouraging the unusual attention being given to the Bible.

But this is not the last church. There is one more church with a very different type of experience.

[7] LAODICEA > LUKEWARM
1900-TODAY

10.   How are these people described?

> *"And to the angel of the church of the Laodiceans write, These things says the Amen, the Faithful and True Witness, the Beginning of the creation of God: I know your works, that you are neither cold nor hot. I could wish you were cold or hot. So then, because you are lukewarm, and neither cold nor hot, I will vomit you out of My mouth. Because you say, I am rich, have become wealthy, and have need of*

> *nothing --- and do not know that you are wretched, miserable, poor, blind, and naked --- I counsel you to buy from Me gold refined in the fire, that you may be rich; and white garments, that you may be clothed, that the shame of your nakedness may not be revealed, and anoint your eyes with eye salve, that you may see." Revelation 3:14-18.*

Jesus' opinion of these Christians is not very complementary. He describes them as **LUKEWARM**, feeling very self-sufficient and unconcerned about their spiritual welfare.

In general, Christianity today fits well the picture drawn here. A preoccupation with the materialism of this modern age has taken its toll on the relationship people have with Christ and His Word. We have now arrived at the end of this prophecy, but not yet at the end of time. In the vision that follows, John will be shown what these Laodicean Christians will face "after this." Revelation 4:1.

If this prophecy tells us anything, it tells us with dramatic clarity that we are now living in momentous times. The end of this world is approaching, and we could easily be the generation that passes through the "time of the end" events and witness the arrival of Christ back to this earth. For this reason, the book of Revelation, which is a reliable manual for navigating through those approaching events, is of intense interest to us. It is imperative, not optional, that we understand this last book of the Bible. We are the generation for which it was originally written. Our immediate future and eternal life depends upon it.

QUIZ FOR LESSON NO. 2

Beginning with this lesson a simple, five-point quiz will be offered. These quizzes will review the main important points of the material covered. They will be helpful for students to refresh their minds concerning these points, as well as to correct anything they have misunderstood. The answers to all quizzes may be found at the end of this book.

TRUE OR FALSE

1. There are eight churches mentioned in this prophetic series.

2. The name of the last church is Laodicea.

3. These churches represent the spiritual experience of Christians from John's time to the end-time.

4. Immoral Nicolaitans were never accepted by any of the churches.

5. The name of the Old Testament woman mentioned in the Thyatira church was Naomi.

Revelation's Table of Contents
Lesson No. 3

The New Vision

The prophecy of the seven churches is limited to the first three chapters of Revelation. Beginning with Chapter 4, verse 1, it is clear that John is given a second vision. This new vision will contain altogether new material than the material of the seven churches.

1. When were the things of this new vision to take place?

   "After these things I looked, and behold, a door standing open in heaven. And the first voice which I heard was like a trumpet speaking with me, saying, Come up here, and I will show you things which must take place after this." Revelation 4:1.

John is told that the things (events) of this new vision would occur **AFTER THIS (THESE THINGS)**, referring to the things of the seven churches. Therefore, rather than before or during the seven churches, these things would "occur subsequent to or follow the seven churches.

The words, "these things" and "after this," refer to the things pictured in the previous vision of the seven churches. All of those things pictured there have already taken place as far as we are concerned, and now Jesus will show John the amazing final events of the time of the end --- events that are about to transpire in our near future.

This new prophecy is also divided into seven segments. It is commonly referred to as the prophecy of the seven seals. Chapters 4 and 5 picture a single introductory scene to those seals.

2. What does John notice in God's hand?

   "And I saw in the right hand of Him who sat on the throne a scroll written inside and on the back, sealed with seven seals. Then I saw a strong angel proclaiming with a loud voice, Who is worthy to open the scroll and to loose its seals? And no one in heaven or on the earth or under the earth was able to open the scroll, or to look at it. So I wept much, because no one was found worthy to open and read the scroll, or to look at it. But one of the elders said to me, do not weep. Behold, the Lion of the tribe of

Judah, the Root of David, has prevailed to open the scroll and to loose its seven seals." Revelation 5:1-5.

The main feature of this prophetic vision is **A SCROLL SEALED WITH SEVEN SEALS**. These seals are the center of attention and, as each one is opened something happens. Revelation 4:1 assures us that what happens are things that will take place after the seven churches.

Table of Contents

Near the front of most books and magazines is a page entitled, "Table of Contents." The information on this particular page contains a brief and orderly list of what is inside the book or magazine. Revelation is laid out much the same way. As we shall see in our study, the seven seals will give us a brief description of the final events of the time of the end. Each of the seven seals will be amazingly brief, leaving us wishing for more details. We need not despair, however, for the remainder of the book of Revelation will discuss each of these seven events in more detail and in the same order. Thus, this vision of the seven seals becomes a kind of "table of contents" for the remainder of the book.

In this lesson we will survey briefly these seven seals, so as to become familiar with their details. In subsequent lessons we will study each individual seal in great detail, allowing the subsequent chapters that match each seal to reveal to us a more elaborate picture of each event that is just ahead in our future.

3.   What color was the first horse?

> *"Now I saw when the Lamb opened one of the seals, and I heard one of the four living creatures saying with a voice like thunder, Come and see. And I looked, and behold, a white horse. He who sat on it had a bow; and a crown was given to him, and he went out conquering and to conquer." Revelation 6:1 ,2.*

The color of this first horse is **WHITE**. The color of each horse in this prophetic series reveals the nature of the event symbolized. The weapon in the hand of each horse's rider is also significant.

4.   What does the color white represent in Revelation?

> *"You have a few names even in Sardis who have not defiled their garments; and they shall walk with Me in white, for they are worthy.*

He who overcomes shall be clothed in white garments, and I will not blot out his name from the Book of Life; but I will confess his name before My Father and before His angels." Revelation 3:4, 5.

Here Jesus is using the color white to indicate that a person is **WORTHY** or an **OVERCOMER**. This white horse must represent spiritual victory over sin and a development of good character and godly living. It is clearly a symbol of something positive, rather than negative.

5.   **What weapon does the rider use?**

"And I looked, and behold, a white horse. He who sat on it had a bow; and a crown was given to him, and he went out conquering and to conquer." Revelation 6:2.

The only weapon this rider used to accomplish this tremendous conquering was a **BOW**. This is not referring to a ribbon bow, but to a weapon used with arrows.

Only one person at a time can be conquered with a bow and arrow. No mass destruction is accomplished with such a weapon. This seal pictures a time of amazing, personal, spiritual victories soon to occur. Chapter 7 will provide us with more information about this event.

6.   **What color was the second horse?**

"When He opened the second seal, I heard the second living creature saying, Come and see. Another horse, fiery red, went out. And it was granted to the one who sat on it to take peace from the earth, and that people should kill one another; and there was given to him a great sword." Revelation 6:3, 4.

The color **RED** is clearly a color depicting a very negative, rather than a positive event. The mention of the fact that this rider will take peace from the earth and people will be killing each other, confirms our first impression of this rider. It is evident that this red horse depicts bloodshed in a war that will be global in scope. A World War III is indicated here, and Chapters 8-11 will provide great detail about this coming global conflict.

7.   **What is the color of the third horse?**

"When He opened the third seal, I heard the third living creature say, Come and see. So I looked, and behold, a black horse, and he

who sat on it had a pair of scales in his hand. And I heard a voice in the midst of the four living creatures saying, A quart of wheat for a denarius, and three quarts of barley for a denarius; and do not harm the oil and the wine." Revelation 6:5, 6.

This horse is **BLACK**.

What does the black horse rider have in his hand?

This is the only horse rider of the series that does not use a weapon. He is pictured simply as using a **PAIR OF SCALES**.

A pair of scales is not a weapon, but a weighing instrument. In reality, it is used as a testing instrument. This seal represents an important event during the end-time that will test the profession of all. This great test that will be brought to bear upon all was alluded to in Revelation 3:10: "Because you have kept my command to persevere, I also will keep you from the hour of trial which comes upon the whole world, to test those who dwell on the earth." Chapters 12-14 will reveal how this will come about and the results it will produce.

8. **What color was the fourth horse?**

"When He opened the fourth seal, I heard the voice of the fourth living creature saying, Come and see. So I looked, and behold, a pale horse. And the name of him who sat on it was Death, and Hades followed with him. And power was given to them over a fourth of the earth, to kill with sword, with hunger, with death, and by the beasts of the earth." Revelation 6:7, 8.

This horse's color is **PALE**. Since the color of each horse is a key to the experience it represents, we are naturally inquisitive about the unusual color of this horse. The English word, "pale" does not do justice to the meaning of the Greek word.

The very strong meaning of this Greek word translated "pale," is brought out in many modern translations by such expressions as "ashy pale," "sickly green," or "ashen."

This is not a normal color, but one of disease and death. Chapters 15 and 16 will unfold to us the nature of this horrible disease and who will be the targets of these plagues.

9. What did John see when the fifth seal was opened?

    "When He opened the fifth seal, I saw under the altar the souls of those who had been slain for the word of God and for the testimony which they held. And they cried with a loud voice, saying, How long, O Lord, holy and true, until You judge and avenge our blood on those who dwell on the earth? Then a white robe was given to each of them; and it was said to them that they should rest a little while longer, until both the number of their fellow servants and their brethren, who would be killed as they were, was completed." Revelation 6:9-11.

When the fifth seal is opened there are no more horses that gallop forth. Instead John sees **PRAYING MARTYRS**, represented as being under an altar.

Over past centuries many have paid for their faith with their own lives. We call these victims "martyrs." Martyrdom in Christianity is different from martyrdom in Islam. These Christians did not die trying to kill others who disagreed with them, but were innocent victims of violence because of their faith.

10. What were they asking God to do?

    "And they cried with a loud voice, saying, How long, O Lord, holy and true, until You judge and avenge our blood on those who dwell on the earth?" Revelation 6:10.

Their prayer was, **"AVENGE OUR BLOOD."** Their focus was upon their murderers. They were pleading for God to bring them to justice. Chapters 17 and 18 will reveal just who these murderers are and how God will answer the prayer of these victims of violence.

11. When the sixth seal was broken, what climactic event did John see?

    "I looked when He opened the sixth seal, and behold, there was a great earthquake; and the sun became black as sackcloth of hair, and the moon became like blood. And the stars of heaven fell to the earth, as a fig tree drops its late figs when it is shaken by a mighty wind. Then the sky receded as a scroll when it is rolled up, and every mountain and island was moved out of its place. And the kings of the earth, the great men, the rich men, the command-

ers, the mighty men, every slave and every free man, hid themselves in the caves and in the rocks of the mountains, and said to the mountains and rocks, Fall on us and hide us from the face of Him who sits on the throne and from the wrath of the Lamb! For the great day of His wrath has come, and who is able to stand?" Revelation 6:12-17.

Symbolism is set aside in the account here, and vivid, literal language is used to describe **CHRIST'S ARRIVAL** into the atmosphere surrounding our planet. A series of supernatural, catastrophic events lead up to the invasion of the earth's atmosphere by Christ Himself. This arrival of Christ in the sky is witnessed by the entire world. Revelation 1:7 also indicates this.

Chapter 19 will elaborate and expand upon the picture briefly given here, of the return of Christ in power and great glory to planet earth. This seven-fold prophecy does not end with the second coming of Christ. There is still one more major event Revelation wants to picture for us. There is a final seal --- a seventh one.

12.   When the seventh seal was broken, what happened?

"When He opened the seventh seal, there was silence in heaven for about half an hour." Revelation 8:1.

This seal is most unique of all the seven seals. Its main event is a period of **SILENCE**, and it will occur **IN HEAVEN**. We are also informed about its duration: **ABOUT HALF-AN-HOUR**.

This seal is separated from the other six seals, because it has something to do **with** the time of the end, but not **during** the time of the end. It actually occurs after the arrival of Christ to earth, which naturally concludes the time of the end.

This is the shortest time prophecy in the Bible. Something of compelling interest must be involved to cause such far-flung silence throughout the universe. Chapters 20-22 will make it clear to us.

SUMMARY

In this survey of the seven seals, we have actually received a brief overview of the rest of the book of Revelation. These short, cryptic, thumbnail sketches of end-time events whet our appetite to push forward into the main part of this book to get clearer insights into each one of these seven momentous events of the time of the end. Since the seven seals act as a kind of table of contents for the rest of the book, we will expect to get clarification for each of these events in the same order that they are represented in these seals. Studying the chart below will help you to see clearly how the seven seals are related to the rest of the book of Revelation.

SUMMARY

Table of Contents	Contents
1- White Horse	Chapter 7
2- Red Horse	Chapters 8-11
3- Black Horse	Chapters 12-14
4- Pale Green Horse	Chapters 15-16
5- Praying Martyrs	Chapters 17-18
6- Second Coming of Christ	Chapter 19
7- Half-Hour of Silence	Chapters 20-22

QUIZ FOR LESSON NO. 3

Choose a color from the list below that matches each seal:

> ORANGE
> BLUE
> BLACK
> PURPLE
> PALE GREEN
> WHITE
> RED

1. Color of the first horse
   (Spiritual Revival)

2. Color of the second horse
   (Global Warfare)

3. Color of the third horse
   (Dark Time of Tribulation)

4. Color of the fourth horse
   (Disease and Sickness)

5. Color of the robes given to the praying martyrs of the fifth seal.

Earth's Final Revival [THE FIRST SEAL]
Lesson No. 4

Our study of Revelation will be less confusing if we always keep in mind how the book is organized. In the previous lessons we discovered the basic outline of this book, and we will now review it before continuing our investigation of this fascinating portion of Scripture.

The book can be divided up into segments characterized by time:

[1] Chapters 1-3 contain a "bridge" prophecy, made up of seven parts. It begins in John's day and stretches into the future from his time. It "locates" the segment of time that is the main focus of Revelation --- the time of the end. This prophecy covers a period of time approximately 2,000 years in length.

[2] Chapters 4-6 contain a "table of contents," briefly picturing the seven major events of that "time of the end." We have surveyed that list in the previous lesson and become acquainted with the language and imagery employed.

[3] Chapters 7-19 contain details, background information, and additional facts that will explain and bring clearly to our minds the nature of those seven major events, in the identical order in which they were first presented in the "table of contents." This period of time is not a long one. It is measured in months rather than years.

[4] Chapters 20-22 deal with the events of a period that will last a little more than 1,000 years. It is the seventh of the "last day events," but separated out from the seven, because it technically occurs after the second coming of Christ, which concludes the time of the end.

To understand the nature of the final events of this time of the end, we will now begin the study of each of these seven seals. We will also drawing upon information from Revelation's subsequent chapters that relate to each seal.

We will always begin by reviewing the facts revealed in the seals themselves, then moving on to the chapter(s) that illuminate the details about the event portrayed.

The Color

1. What is the color of the horse in the first seal?

> *"Now I saw when the Lamb opened one of the seals, and I heard one of the four living creatures saying with a voice like thunder, Come and see. And I looked, and behold, a white horse. He who sat on it had a bow; and a crown was given to him, and he went out conquering and to conquer."* Revelation 6:1, 2.

The color of each horse indicates the nature of the event it represents. Each horse's color will be different since it portrays a different event. The color of this first horse is **WHITE**. While John does not reveal the identity of the rider, we will notice with this and subsequent horses that the color of the animal is helpful to identify rider's character, which in turn hints as to his identity. Some Bible students interpret this rider as the Antichrist, but later on the book pictures the Antichrist as riding on a "scarlet beast," not a white one (see Revelation 17:3).

2. What do white garments on people represent?

> *"You have a few names even in Sardis who have not defiled their garments; and they shall walk with Me in white, for they are worthy. He who overcomes shall be clothed in white garments, and I will not blot out his name from the Book of Life; but I will confess his name before My Father and before His angels."* Revelation 3:4, 5.

These people are pictured as dressed in white because they are **WORTHY** and are **OVERCOMERS**. They are not bad or evil, they are clearly born-again believers. The rider on this white horse must be Christ Himself, and this conclusion is in harmony with the book of Revelation, which later on is pictured as riding on a white horse (see Revelation 19:11-13).

3. What did the rider of this horse achieve?

> *"And I looked, and behold, a white horse. He who sat on it had a bow; and a crown was given to him, and he went out conquering and to conquer." Revelation 6:2.*

Something unusually successful is pictured here. The rider's work is described as **CONQUERING AND TO CONQUER**. It appears to be a very positive achievement, not the debilitating, oppressive accomplishment of an evil despot. This is all the information we are given for this seal, with nothing more given to aid us in interpreting this cryptic symbolism. We need not despair, however, for the very first segment of Revelation which follows these seven seals is Chapter 7, and in it we will find answers that fit and illuminate this white horse event.

Chapter 7

4. In this explanatory chapter of the first seal, how were victorious believers clothed?

> *"After these things I looked, and behold, a great multitude which no one could number, of all nations, tribes, peoples, and tongues, standing before the throne and before the Lamb, clothed with white robes, with palm branches in their hands." Revelation 7:9.*

Here we see people, not horses, in **WHITE**. Furthermore, we notice that a global, worldwide, spiritual movement produced this group. This is not a small group, restricted to one nation. It is an innumerable and multi-national mass of humanity. Clearly, the results of a world-wide revival is pictured here.

5. How did they get that way?

> *"Then one of the elders answered, saying to me, Who are these arrayed in white robes, and where did they come from? And I said to him, Sir, you know. So he said to me, These are the ones who come out of the great tribulation, and washed their robes and made them white in the blood of the Lamb." Revelation 7:13, 14.*

Their garments were not that way originally. A great change happened to them. They had to be washed to achieve this purity. Their robes were **MADE WHITE IN THE BLOOD OF THE LAMB**.

Notice that they are identified as last-day Christians, because they came through "the great tribulation." This was not all the saved of all ages, but only a certain specific group. They must be Laodiceans (the last day Christians of the seven churches), who accepted Jesus' advice in Revelation 3:18: "I counsel you to buy from Me . . . white garments, that you may be clothed." The religious experience of those Laodiceans was portrayed originally as being "wretched, miserable, poor, blind, and naked." What a change has come over them!

6. **For us to be "washed in His blood," what two things does Jesus do for us?**

"But if we walk in the light as He is in the light, we have fellowship with one another, and the blood of Jesus Christ His Son cleanses us from all sin. If we say that we have no sin, we deceive ourselves, and the truth is not in us. If we confess our sins, He is faithful and just to forgive us our sins and to cleanse us from all unrighteousness." I John 1:7-9.

Jesus **[1] FORGIVES OUR SINS**, and **[2] CLEANSES US FROM ALL UNRIGHTEOUSNESS**. The forgiveness of sins is for what we have done wrong in the past. The Bible does not suggest we can obtain forgiveness in advance for what we will do wrong in the future. Such an arrangement has been advocated by Christians in the past, and is called "indulgences."

It's wonderful news that Jesus will forgive and wipe clean our past, but an even more precious promise is that He offers to cleanse us from all unrighteousness. This involves the present and the future, and portrays what the Bible calls "overcoming" and "victory over sin."

These ideas are portrayed by the biblical metaphor of coming under the blood of Jesus. The blood in our physical bodies has a two-fold task. The blood carries away from the tissues and cells of the body toxins and waste that would hinder and harm the bodily functions, if not removed.

However, that is only one part of the blood's task. The other is to infuse the tissues and cells with nutrients and life-giving elements that help the body ward off destructive diseases.

The Forehead Mark

7. In this explanatory chapter of the first seal, what will be placed on the foreheads of a specific group?

"After these things I saw four angels standing at the four corners of the earth, holding the four winds of the earth, that the wind should not blow on the earth, on the sea, or on any tree. Then I saw another angel ascending from the east, having the seal of the living God. And he cried with a loud voice to the four angels to whom it was granted to harm the earth and the sea, saying, Do not harm the earth, the sea, or the trees till we have sealed the servants of our God on their foreheads." Revelation 7:1-3.

THE SEAL OF THE LIVING GOD is not placed on these people by other human beings, but by God's own angels. Seals are used in two ways in the book of Revelation. There is a "closure" seal which is a mechanism used to secure something against tampering by unauthorized individuals. This is the kind of seals John saw on the book sealed with seven seals in heaven. Then there is the "approval" seal. This seal is affixed to documents or products, to attest, affirm, or approve of that on which it is placed.

It is this second use of a seal that is intended in Chapter 7 of Revelation. These people will have so fully opened their lives to Jesus, to obey and follow Him, that His special seal of approval is placed upon them.

Their number is mentioned in verse 4 as being 144,000. There is not enough information here to reveal precisely who these marked people are, but we are told later in Revelation that they are the "firsfruits" (Revelation 14:4), indicating more than these will be saved in this great spiritual awakening that is soon to take place. The first group, 144,000 in number, is apparently the initial group, much as Jesus used just 12 disciples as a start-up group, resulting in an innumerable company of future disciples.

8.   **What is this "seal" mark on their foreheads?**

> *"Then I looked, and behold, a Lamb standing on Mount Zion, and with Him one hundred and forty-four thousand, having His Father's name written on their foreheads." Revelation 14:1.*

This special seal is otherwise described as **THE FATHER'S NAME**. Just as in these modern times, the word "name" is used in the Bible to mean "character." For instance, we use such expressions as "that company has a good name," or "she has made quite a name for herself."

9.   **Who gets involved in sealing believers?**

> *"And do not grieve the Holy Spirit of God, by whom you were sealed for the day of redemption. Let all bitterness, wrath, anger, clamor, and evil speaking be put away from you, with all malice. And be ye kind to one another, tenderhearted, forgiving one another, even as God in Christ forgave you." Ephesians 4:30-32.*

THE HOLY SPIRIT has a lot to do with this sealing process. Paul's words here indicate that if we are to be sealed we must undergo a radical change in our thinking, which involves our attitudes, plans, mind-set, etc. Only then can God's seal be placed upon our foreheads, where our mind is. A radical change of heart, as well as a change in our outward behavior, is the only condition worthy of that seal of approval from God Himself. The Holy Spirit does not do this suddenly and unannounced. His work in us is a progressive one, a process.

10.   **What is the three-step process?**

> *"In Him you also trusted, after you heard the word of truth, the gospel of your salvation; in whom also, having believed, you were sealed with the Holy Spirit of promise." Ephesians 1:13.*

The process the Holy Spirit follows has a distinct pattern. First, we must **HEAR THE WORD OF TRUTH**. We need some information on which to decide and act, and the source of that information is the Bible. Second, we must **BELIEVE THE GOSPEL**. Knowledge alone, while essential, does not save us. It is our reaction or response to what we know that is the deciding factor, and our actions reveal our belief or disbelief. Last, we are **SEALED WITH THE HOLY SPIRIT**.

The Word of God plays a central role in the process. To believe just any old thing will not automatically bring us salvation. Deception and falsehood will abound in the time of the end, but we can only be sanctified by truth. John 17:17. Make sure what you believe is truth that can be supported by the Bible.

The Holy Spirit

Since it is so clear from the Bible that the Holy Spirit is closely involved with last-day believers receiving the seal of God, we are deeply interested in how Revelation and other Scriptures picture the activities of the Holy Spirit in this special end time.

11. **In the introductory vision to the seven seals, where does John see the Holy Spirit, represented by seven lamps?**

    "And from the throne proceeded lightnings, thunderings, and voices. Seven lamps of fire were burning before the throne, which are the seven Spirits of God." Revelation 4:5.

The English translation of this text sounds like there are seven, not just one, Holy Spirits, but everywhere else in previous Scripture He is described as one single, divine individual, not seven. Perhaps this vision pictures the Holy Spirit in His sevenfold work, as enumerated in Isaiah 11:2.

What is very clear, however, is the location in which the Holy Spirit is pictured. John notices that He is **BEFORE THE THRONE**.

12. **Later in that same vision, where does John see the Holy Spirit, represented by seven eyes?**

    "And I looked, and behold, in the midst of the throne and of the four living creatures, and in the midst of the elders, stood a Lamb as though it had been slain, having seven horns and seven eyes, which are the seven Spirits of God sent out into all the earth." Revelation 5:6.

Now the Holy Spirit is no longer "before the throne," but He is **SENT OUT INTO ALL THE WORLD**. There is a clear representation here of the movement of the Holy Spirit sometime after the experiences of the seven churches have been completed, and just prior to the events of the seven seals.

Chapters 5 and 6 are all one vision, revealing to John things that were to happen in heaven before the opening of any of the seals. John is shown a special movement of the Holy Spirit, referred to in an Old Testament prophecy. Let us look at that prophecy now.

13.   Upon whom will the Holy Spirit be poured?

> *"And it shall come to pass afterward that I will pour out My Spirit on all flesh; your sons and your daughters shall prophesy, your old men shall dream dreams, your young men shall see visions. And also on My menservants and on My maidservants I will pour out My Spirit in those days. And I will show wonders in the heavens and in the earth: blood and fire and pillars of smoke. The sun shall be turned into darkness, and the moon into blood, before the coming of the great and awesome day of the Lord." Joel 2:28-31.*

Did you notice the extent to which the Holy Spirit targets His efforts? **ON ALL FLESH**, is precisely, although in different words, the same as "sent out into all the world." The results of this outpouring of the Spirit will be a deep and far reaching spiritual revival among mankind. It is pictured thus in the following verse of Joel's prophecy.

14.   What will be the result?

> *"And it shall come to pass that whoever calls on the name of the Lord shall be saved. For in Mount Zion and in Jerusalem there shall be deliverance, as the Lord has said, Among the remnant whom the Lord calls." Joel 2:32.*

MANY WILL BE SAVED. It will be a time of many turning to the Lord. This world will have never seen such a spiritual revival as pictured here. This special outpouring of God's Spirit upon the earth is likened to the rain seasons in Palestine. Just after planting time in the spring, a rainy season starts the growth. Just before harvest time in the fall, a heavy rainy season returns, which fully ripens the grain and makes it ready for harvest.

15.   What does the Bible call these two rainy seasons?

"Therefore be patient, brethren, until the coming of the Lord. See how the farmer waits for the precious fruit of the earth, waiting patiently for it until it receives the early and latter rain." James 5:7.

There are two rainy seasons mentioned here in this text: **EARLY AND LATTER RAIN.** We can read in the book of Acts about the amazing spiritual awakening of the people when God's Spirit was poured out at Pentecost   That was the "early rain." We have yet to see a similar, but more far-reaching, spiritual awakening in these last days. That "early" outpouring of the Spirit shook all of old Jerusalem with spiritual energy. The "latter" outpouring of God's Spirit is symbolized by this rider on a white horse, going out "conquering and to conquer." It will impact "all nations, tribes, peoples, and tongues"(Revelation 7:9).

If we want to be ready for God to place His seal of approval upon us someday, we must now [1] Open our hearts to accept Jesus and believe that His blood can forgive and cleanse us from all our sins; and [2] search God's Word to make sure that no false beliefs or ideas are entertained, so that we can be sanctified by His truth found there.

QUIZ FOR LESSON NO. 4

Choose one right answer:

1. Color of the horse in the first seal:
   (A) Black
   (B) White
   (C) Red

2. How many nations will have a chance to accept the gospel in the end-time?
   (A) A few nations
   (B) All nations
   (C) Nations of the West

3. When the first seal is opened, the Holy Spirit:
   (A) Goes back to heaven
   (B) Stays in heaven
   (C) Is sent out to all the earth

4. Where will God's seal be placed?
   (A) On the forehead
   (B) On the hand
   (C) On an arm band

5. What must we accept in order to receive God's seal?
   (A) Any belief, but be sincere
   (B) God's Word of Truth
   (C) Falsehoods and lies

The Point of No Return
Lesson No. 5

Having just concluded our study of the first seal, we would normally turn our attention to the second seal. However, before we do, it is vital that we first understand a very important event pictured in Revelation and in other passages of Scripture.

The Benchmark Event

In the book of Revelation there is pictured an end-time event having such extreme importance and far-reaching consequences, we call it a "benchmark" event. A benchmark is a point of reference from which everything else is viewed, understood, or done. It is unmovable and influences all that is associated with it. Students of Bible prophecy call this benchmark event "the close of human probation." Being aware of it is vital to our study of Revelation.

What Causes It?

1. What was used in heaven to process the prayers of those praying on earth?

    "Then another angel, having a golden censer, came and stood at the altar. He was given much incense, that he should offer it with the prayers of all the saints upon the golden altar which was before the throne. And the smoke of the incense, with the prayers of the saints, ascended before God from the angel's hand." Revelation 8:3, 4.

The instrument this angel used was **A GOLDEN CENSER**. This imagery comes from the Old Testament sanctuary service, where the priests were instructed to offer this incense every day of the year (see Exodus 30:7, 8).

In the Old Testament a human being did this on a golden altar in the earthly sanctuary. In Revelation an angel was shown doing this upon a golden altar in heaven. Both represented the work Jesus Christ does for us on a daily basis, which is essential for our salvation. Hebrews 7:25 explains this to us. "Therefore He (Christ) is also able to save to the uttermost those who come to God through Him, since He always lives to make intercession for them." The book of Hebrews calls this a work of "intercession."

2.   **Because of Jesus' priestly intercession in heaven, what is available to us?**

> *"Seeing then that we have a great High Priest who has passed through the heavens, Jesus the Son of God, let us hold fast our confession. For we do not have a High Priest who cannot sympathize with our weaknesses, but was in all points tempted as we are, yet without sin. Let us therefore come boldly to the throne of grace, that we may obtain mercy and find grace to help in time of need." Hebrews 4:14-16.*

Jesus' work on the cross did something for us, without any participation on our part. His death paid the penalty of our wrongdoing. He died for our sins, "once for all." But Jesus' work in heaven for us now is described as an ongoing work that necessitates our cooperation and participation. It is described as **MERCY AND GRACE TO HELP US**. This grace that Jesus dispenses *helps* us; it does not do everything for us. Nevertheless, it is extremely essential, for Jesus said, "Without me you can do nothing." John 15:5. To depict this on-going dependence on Christ, twice each day, morning and evening, the Old Testament priests were instructed to officiate with incense at the golden altar of the sanctuary.

Throwing away the censer indicates that Christ's mediatory work is done. Therefore, unrepentant sinners on earth no longer have intercession available to them from Christ. Since sinful man cannot save himself, the end result is that man's character and eternal destiny from that point on is irreversible. The Bible often pictures such a possibility.

3.   **What was suddenly done with the censer?**

> *"Then the angel took the censer, filled it with fire from the altar, and threw it to the earth. And there were noises, thunderings, lightnings, and an earthquake." Revelation 8:5, 6.*

It was violently **THROWN TO THE EARTH.** It was not accidently dropped, or temporarily laid aside. It was deliberately and permanently thrown away. This signals that heavenly intercession for people who are seeking salvation is permanently ended.

This is not the one and only time in the Bible that reveals a complete cessation of opportunity for people to be saved by Christ. There are many biblical examples portraying that this will happen in the time of the end.

Bible Examples

4. When Noah and the animals entered the ark, when did God shut the door?

> *"On the very same day Noah and Noah's sons, Shem, Ham, and Japheth, and Noah's wife and the three wives of his sons with them, entered the ark---they and every beast after its kind, all cattle after their kind, every creeping thing that creeps on the earth after its kind, and every bird after its kind, every bird of every sort. And they went into the ark to Noah, two by two, of all flesh in which is the breath of life. So those that entered, male and female of all flesh, went in as God had commanded him; and the Lord shut him in." Genesis 7:13-16*

What a day in history that was! In just one 24-hour period of time, Noah and his family moved into the ark and began finding a place for all the animals. When all of this was accomplished **THE SAME DAY**, the Bible says that God shut the massive entrance door to that vessel.

When that door was shut by God Himself, those who were saved inside could not come out, and those who were outside could not come in. Their destiny was sealed and irreversible. That very evening opportunity for anyone who did not obey God and enter the ark was gone forever. Their time of probation, their time to prove their belief in and obedience to God expired, and their awful destiny was fixed.

5.   How much time passed before the flood came?

> *"So Noah, with his sons, his wife, and his sons' wives, went into the ark because of the waters of the flood. Of clean animals, of animals that are unclean, of birds, and of everything that creeps on the earth, two by two they went into the ark to Noah, male and female, as God had commanded Noah. And it came to pass after seven days that the waters of the flood were on the earth." Genesis 7:7-10.*

SEVEN DAYS passed before anything unusual happened. There was a short period of time that passed uneventfully. Yet, for the unbelieving people, the end of their opportunity to be saved from the flood came sometime before the flood actually arrived. No last-minute change of mind was possible.

6.   Jesus compares the days of Noah to what other event?

> *"And as it was in the days of Noah, so it will be also in the days of the Son of Man. They ate, they drank, they married wives, they were given in marriage, until the day that Noah entered into the ark, and the flood came and destroyed them all." Luke 17:26, 27.*

Jesus says that a similar thing would happen in **THE DAYS OF THE SON OF MAN**. A couple of verses previous to this statement (verse 24) Jesus was referring to the day when He would return to this earth as "His day."

7.   What did Jesus say will keep some from being saved in the kingdom of heaven?

> *"Then one said to Him, Lord, are there few who are saved? And He said to them, Strive to enter through the narrow gate, for many, I say to you, will seek to enter and will not be able. When once the Master of the house has risen up and shut the door, and*

you begin to stand outside and knock at the door, saying, Lord, Lord, open for us, and He will answer and say to you, I do not know you, where you are from." Luke 13:23-25.

WHEN THE DOOR IS SHUT these people will seek entrance. Here are people whose opportunity to get into the kingdom of God is closed, but they are represented as living on, actually trying to get in, but meeting with complete failure and finding it too late. This is another biblical account of a time when, once the door to salvation is shut, no one else will be able to enter.

8. In a parable Jesus told about a wedding, what did He say was done when everyone went in?

"And while they went to buy, the bridegroom came, and those who were ready went in with him to the wedding; and the door was shut." Matthew 25:10.

In this wedding parable Jesus makes a prominent point that when the wedding began **THE DOOR WAS SHUT**.

9. When did others come to seek entrance?

"Afterward the other virgins came also, saying, Lord, Lord, open to us! But he answered and said, Assuredly, I say to you, I do not know you." Matthew 25:11, 12.

When the door was shut, the group pictured came **AFTERWARD**. Jesus told this parable to illustrate what will happen at His second coming. Verse 13 says: "Watch therefore, for you know neither the day nor the hour in which the Son of Man is coming."

The late-comers represent those who will procrastinate and put off their spiritual preparations, planning to get serious at the last moment. To their horror, they learn that they have no second chance.

These numerous illustrations from the teachings of Jesus make it apparent that He saw in the future, near the end of time, that there would be drawn a final "line in the sand," a moment beyond which there would be no further opportunity to repent and be converted. Now there is still probationary time for us, yet soon, sometime just prior to the end of all things, that door of probation will be closed to the human race.

Revelation

In the book of Revelation this special event is pictured symbolically by the casting down of the heavenly censer. Later in the book, it is described in clear, literal language.

10. **What unique and unusual word does Jesus make in the time of the end?**

> *"And he said to me, Do not seal the words of the prophecy of this book, for the time is at hand. He who is unjust, let him be unjust still; he who is filthy, let him be filthy still; he who is righteous, let him be righteous still; he who is holy, let him be holy still." Revelation 22:10, 11.*

Jesus used one word to reveal that after a certain time no one will change in character. Four times the word **STILL** is used. No repentance by wrongdoers and no backsliding by believers will occur. Whatever people are, in character, is what they remain. There is no second chance for them.

11. **What follows soon after?**

> *"And behold, I am coming quickly, and My reward is with Me, to give to every one according to his works." Revelation 22:12.*

JESUS' COMING follows this declaration. Note that this finalizing of one's character and eternal destiny does not occur *after*, or even *at*, but sometime *shortly before* the arrival of Christ back to earth. This means that when Christ returns, all will receive their reward on the same day, not some then and others after seven years.

How Soon Before?

Does the Bible give us any indication as to how much time will pass between the close of human probation and the arrival of Christ? While no precise amount of time is revealed to us, yet the book of Revelation gives us a general idea.

12.   What will happen shortly after the censer is discarded?

> *"So the seven angels who had the seven trumpets prepared themselves to sound." Revelation 8:6.*

THE SEVEN TRUMPETS PREPARE TO SOUND after the casting away of the heavenly censer. Revelation is trying to show us that when heavenly intercession for mankind ceases, it is not the end of the world. There are still momentous events to take place, symbolized by the seven trumpets that follow. While we are not told how much time will pass while these trumpet events occur, there is one time clue in the trumpet series.

13.   How much time is mentioned in the fifth trumpet?

> *"And they were not given authority to kill them, but to torment them for five months. Their torment was like the torment of a scorpion when it strikes a man." Revelation 9:5.*

That is considerably more time than the brief seven days God decreed for Noah's time. We are told that this fifth trumpet will take **FIVE MONTHS**. The passing of this amount of time still does not take us up to the actual second coming of Christ and the end of the world. Two more trumpet events are still to follow. A study of the seven trumpets will reveal that the exact amount of time elapsing between the close of human probation and the arrival of Christ can be just a number of months. What a momentous time that will be!

QUIZ FOR LESSON NO. 5

Yes or No:

1. People can repent and be saved after Jesus arrives.

2. People can repent and be saved the moment they see Jesus coming in the sky.

3. People can be saved right now.

4. Seven trumpets sound before probation closes for all.

5. Five minutes before Jesus arrives, probation will end for all.

Earth's Final War [THE SECOND SEAL]
Lesson No. 6

We are now ready to study the second seal. When it opens, another horse appears, but this second horse differs markedly in its color from the first one.

The Red Horse

1. **What does the rider use to do his work?**

    "When He opened the second seal, I heard the second living creature saying, Come and see. Another horse, fiery red, went out. And it was granted to the one who sat on it to take peace from the earth, and that people should kill one another; and there was given to him a great sword." Revelation 6:3,4.

This rider wields **A GREAT SWORD**. This weapon reveals that the red horse depicts violence, bloodshed, and strife.

2. **What will people do at this time?**

    ". . . that people should kill one another." Revelation 6:4.

They will **KILL ONE ANOTHER**. A reciprocal pronoun is used here. It means the action indicated comes from both sides, not just one. Persecution is violence from one side only. Warfare is a reciprocal action, violence comes from both sides.

3. **What impact will this rider have on the earth?**

    "And it was granted to the one who sat on it to take peace from the earth . . ." Revelation 6:4.

This conflict will be global in extent. It will not be some local or private political issue between one or two nations. This rider will **TAKE PEACE FROM THE EARTH**.

We have no more information from this seal's description with regard to the nature of this global war, which will break out in the future. Since the seals are but a brief table of contents, we can be assured that a more elaborate description of this military violence will be given to us farther on in the book of Revelation. But how can we locate this information in the subsequent portion of Revelation?

We have learned earlier in our studies that these "horse seals" are but a brief sketch of end-time events that Revelation will later expand upon. A book's subject matter always appears in the same order as is listed in the table of contents. Revelation's book is no exception.

Seal	Explanation
1 – White Horse	Chapter 7
2 – Red Horse	Chapters 8-11

Since the white horse of the first seal is explained in Chapter 7, it is logical to look in the following chapters for Revelation's detailed treatment of the second seal which depicts a global war. Chapters 8-11 will provide amazing details of that war. But before we examine those chapters, we will notice some clues as to the timing of this world conflict.

When Will It Begin?

4. **What horse appears before the red horse?**

    "And I looked, and behold, a white horse. He who sat on it had a bow; and a crown was given to him, and he went out conquering and to conquer." Revelation 6:2.

This red horse is the second, not the first horse. It does not ride forth until the **WHITE HORSE** appears, which depicts a global revival resulting in God placing His seal of approval upon believers. Since that has not yet taken place, it is safe to say that the global warfare of the red horse has not yet occurred. Thus, we can conclude that the global conflict represented by this red war horse was not World War II, nor any other past conflict. The world war depicted by this second seal is still forthcoming.

5. **What will God do to believers before He allows the winds of strife to harm the earth?**

    "After these things I saw four angels standing at the four corners of the earth, holding the four winds of the earth, that the wind should not blow on the earth, on the sea, or on any tree. Then I

saw another angel ascending from the east, having the seal of the living God. And he cried with a loud voice to the four angels to whom it was granted to harm the earth and the sea, saying, Do not harm the earth, the sea, or the trees till we have sealed the servants of our God on their foreheads." Revelation 7:1-3.

We studied about this chapter in connection with the first seal. It depicts a global spiritual revival, when believers will be **SEALED ON THEIR FOREHEADS.** The pivotal word is "till." This means that the sealing work revival must be completed before God will allow war of this magnitude to break out. The fact that the wind will blow from the four corners of the earth, rather than from just one area, indicates the global magnitude of this conflict. This is another clue that we must look to our future for the fulfillment of this red horse warfare.

Since we know that the vision of Chapters 8-11 deals with this future global war, we will now study that part of Revelation and find that those details illuminate the red horse of the seven seals.

6. **When the heavenly censer was thrown away, what was blown by seven angels?**

"And I saw the seven angels who stand before God, and to them were given seven trumpets. Then another angel, having a golden censer, came and stood at the altar. He was given much incense, that he should offer it with the prayers of all the saints upon the golden altar which was before the throne. And the smoke of the incense, with the prayers of the saints, ascended before God from the angel's hand. Then the angel took the censer, filled it with fire from the altar, and threw it to the earth. And there were noises, thunderings, lightnings, and an earthquake. So the seven angels who had the seven trumpets prepared themselves to sound." Revelation 8:2-6.

These seven angels were issued **SEVEN TRUMPETS**. Soon we will see that as each of these trumpets is blown, a special phase of a global conflict will break out on earth. Therefore these seven trumpets amplify and illuminate the global conflict of the red horse rider mentioned earlier in the "table of contents" vision (the seven seals).

At the very outset of this vision of the seven trumpets we are given a definite time clue as to just when we can expect this global war. Although the angels were given these trumpets while the censer was being used (see vs. 2), they did nothing with them until they saw the intercessory work cease. When that happens all restraint is removed, and Satan will then plunge this earth into one final, awful conflict.

Trumpets

7. What were trumpets used for in Bible times?

"When you go to war in your land against the enemy who oppresses you, then you shall sound an alarm with the trumpets, and you will be remembered before the Lord your God, and you will be saved from your enemies." Numbers 10:9.

A trumpet does not cause war, but warns of its imminent approach. These trumpets do not reveal what God will do, but what man will do to man. Trumpets were used in Bible times much the same way we use sirens in modern times. They are used **TO SOUND AN ALARM.**

8. What should one do when the war trumpet sounds?

"For if the trumpet makes an uncertain sound, who will prepare for the battle?" I Corinthians 14:8.

When a war trumpet is sounded, it is a call to **PREPARE FOR BATTLE**. God commissions the seven angels to blow their trumpets so that His people can prepare themselves --- not to fight, but to protect themselves from the impending danger. They are blown one at a time, to reveal seven different aspects of the conflict ahead.

TRUMPET NO. 1
VEGETATION

The description of what will happen when each of these trumpets is blown is very detailed. It will help us sort out these details in a meaningful way by noticing three basic items: [1] the weapon used, [2] the target which suffers, and [3] the extent of the damage done.

9. *The first angel sounded: And hail and fire followed, mingled with blood, and they were thrown to the earth. And a third of the trees were burned up, and all green grass was burned up."*
Revelation 8:7.

In this opening salvo of war the weapon that will be used is described as **HAIL, FIRE, AND BLOOD**, the target of this attack is **EARTH, TREES AND GRASS**, and the extent of the damage is that **ONE THIRD OF THEM IS BURNED UP**.

The main target of each of the first four trumpets is not people themselves, but their environment. However, people will suffer as a side effect of the attack. An attack of this kind can easily be carried out by biological or chemical weaponry.

TRUMPET NO. 2
MARINE LIFE

10. *"Then the second angel sounded: And something like a great mountain burning with fire was thrown into the sea, and a third of the sea became blood. And a third of the living creatures in the sea died, and a third of the ships were destroyed." Revelation 8:8, 9.*

The weapon being used here was like nothing he had seen before. He states that it was **SOMETHING LIKE A BURNING MOUNTAIN**. It plunged into **THE SEA**, resulting in **ONE THIRD OF SEA LIFE DESTROYED**. John was witnessing a ball of fire so massive, it appeared to him to look *"something like"* a blazing mountain, but not a literal volcano eruption.

TRUMPET NO. 3
FRESH WATER

11. *"Then the third angel sounded: And a great star fell from heaven, burning like a torch, and it fell on a third of the rivers and on the springs of water. The name of the star is Wormwood. A third of the waters became wormwood, and many men died from the water, because it was made bitter." Revelation 8:10, 11.*

Here John witnessed the weapon being used, a huge flaming missile which he described as **A GREAT BURNING STAR**. It landed upon the **RIVERS AND SPRINGS** as its target, and the resulting damage done was **MANY PEOPLE POISONED**.

A common characteristic of these initial trumpet attacks is that they originate from the sky --- an unknown method of warfare in John's time.

TRUMPET NO. 4
ATMOSPHERE

12. *"Then the fourth angel sounded: And a third of the sun was struck, a third of the moon, and a third of the stars, so that a third of them were darkened. A third of the day did not shine, and likewise the night." Revelation 8:12.*

The targets impacted by this trumpet attack are **THE SUN, MOON AND STARS**. The magnitude of the damage is listed as **ONE THIRD DARKENED**. The weapon used to cause this damage is not mentioned, but it is evident that the air pollution it caused did not disappear, even at night.

TRUMPET NO. 5
ARMY NO. 1

While the first four trumpets depict the use of unmanned weaponry, the last three trumpets describe armies on the attack. There are three distinct armed forces pictured, each using specialized weaponry to accomplish their purpose.

13. *"Then the fifth angel sounded: And I saw a star fallen from heaven to the earth. To him was given the key to the bottomless pit. And he opened the bottomless pit, and smoke arose out of the pit like the smoke of a great furnace. So the sun and the air were darkened because of the smoke of the pit. Then out of the smoke locusts came upon the earth. And to them was given power, as the scorpions of the earth have power. They were commanded not to harm the grass of the earth, or any green thing, or any tree, but only those men who do not have the seal of God on their foreheads. And they were not given authority to kill them, but to torment them for five months. Their torment was like the torment of a scorpion when it strikes a man. In those days men will seek death and will not find it; they will desire to die, and death will flee from them. The shape of the locusts was like horses prepared for battle. On their heads were crowns of something like gold, and their faces were like the faces of men. They had hair like women's hair, and their teeth were like lions' teeth. And they had breastplates like breastplates of iron, and the sound of their wings was like the sound of chariots with many horses running into battle. They had tails like scorpions, and there were stings in their tails. Their power was to hurt men five months. And they had as king over them the angel of the bottomless pit, whose name in He-*

brew is Abaddon, but in Greek he has the name Apollyon." Revelation 9:1-11.

Here we see that this attacking army uses **LOCUST-LIKE MECHANISMS** as its weapons. It does not target mankind in general, but **ALL WITHOUT THE SEAL OF GOD**. The damage it inflicts is most unusual. It produces **A NON-LETHAL TORMENT**.

From the many descriptions John gives them, it is evident that these are not literal locusts or grasshoppers that he is seeing.

[1]   These locusts emerge out of smoke (vs. 3). Literal locusts do not breed in or emerge from smoke. On the contrary, smoke is used to kill them.

[2]   These locusts have a stinging capacity similar to scorpions (vss. 3, 10). Literal locusts have no such ability and are harmless to humans.

[3]   These locusts do not touch any greenery (vs. 4). Literal locusts consume anything within their path that is green.

[4]   These locusts attack only those who do not have the seal of God (vs. 4). Literal locusts do not attack human beings. Even if they did, they have no ability to discern between those who do and those who do not have the seal of God.

Notice the innovative weapons used by this army. Instead of killing, they incapacitate people. These horrifying vehicles and weapons were strange to John, and he desperately tried to describe their unusual features with a multitude of comparisons to things he did understand. It was the best a first-century prophet could do to describe modern instruments of war being shown to him in vision.

TRUMPET NO. 6
ARMY NO. 2

14.   "*Then the sixth angel sounded: And I heard a voice from the four horns of the golden altar which is before God, saying to the sixth angel who had the trumpet, Release the four angels who are bound at the great river Euphrates. So the four angels, who had been prepared for the hour and day and month and year, were released to kill a third of mankind. Now the number of the army of the horsemen was two hundred million; I heard the number of them. And thus I saw the horses in the vision: those who sat on them had breastplates of fiery red, hyacinth blue, and sulfur yellow; and the heads of the horses were like the heads of lions; and out of their*

mouths came fire, smoke, and brimstone. By these three plagues a third of mankind was killed—by the fire and the smoke and the brimstone which came out of their mouths. For their power is in their mouth and in their tails; for their tails are like serpents, having heads; and with them they do harm." Revelation 9:13-19.

The weapons used by this army are **HORSE-LIKE MECHANISMS. MANKIND** is in the cross hairs of this aggressive action, and the staggering result is **ONE-THIRD OF MANKIND KILLED!** We see here another army, greater in number than any in earth's military history. Their weapons are so lethal that a full third of earth's population is annihilated. That red horse rider which represents this global conflict was truly given a *great* sword to take peace from the earth! The present population of our world is around seven billion. Only by nuclear weaponry could a third of mankind be annihilated.

TRUMPET NO. 7
ARMY NO. 3

15.   Who is announced to take control of this world?

"Then the seventh angel sounded: And there were loud voices in heaven, saying, The kingdoms of this world have become the kingdoms of our Lord and of His Christ, and He shall reign forever and ever! And the twenty-four elders who sat before God on their thrones fell on their faces and worshiped God, saying, We give You thanks, O Lord God Almighty, the One who is and who was and who is to come, because you have taken your great power and reigned. The nations were angry, and your wrath has come, and the time of the dead, that they should be judged, and that You should reward Your servants the prophets and the saints, and those who fear Your name, small and great, and should destroy those who destroy the earth." Revelation 11:15-18.

GOD AND CHRIST will exert Their power to take control of this world. Human armies have been fighting to gain world dominance and, in the process, are destroying the earth. It is now God's turn to intervene with the most lethal force of all.

16. What army will help Christ take control of this fighting world?

"Now I saw heaven opened, and behold, a white horse. And He who sat on him was called Faithful and True, and in righteousness He judges and makes war. His eyes were like a flame of fire, and on His head were many crowns. He had a name written that no one knew except Himself. He was clothed with a robe dipped in blood, and His name is called the Word of God. And the armies in heaven, clothed in fine linen, white and clean, followed Him on white horses. Now out of His mouth goes a sharp sword, that with it He should strike the nations. And He Himself will rule them with a rod of iron. He Himself treads the winepress of the fierceness and wrath of Almighty God. And He has on His robe and on His thigh a name written: King of kings and Lord of Lords." Revelation 19:11-16.

This is the third and last army to use force on the earth. It is **THE ARMIES OF HEAVEN**, because this fighting force comes from there. This is the last battle ever to be fought on earth, or even in God's universe. Elsewhere in Revelation it is called the "battle of the great day of God Almighty," or "Armageddon

QUIZ FOR LESSON NO. 6

Choose from this list:
   (A) Takes peace from the earth
   (B) Vegetation
   (C) Atmosphere Pollution
   (D) Marine Life
   (E) Fresh Water Supply

1. The first trumpet targets the earth, trees and grass.

2. The second trumpet targets the sea.

3. The third trumpet targets the rivers and springs of water.

4. The fourth trumpet targets the sun, moon and stars.

5. What is the work of the rider on the fiery red horse?

The Great Tribulation [THE THIRD SEAL]
Lesson No. 7

The Third Horse

1. What appeared when the third seal was broken?

   "When He opened the third seal, I heard the third living creature say, Come and see. So I looked, and behold, a black horse, and he who sat on it had a pair of scales in his hand." Revelation 6:5.

A BLACK HORSE now appears in John's vision. Like the two previous horses, its color carries great significance. The color black represents a very dark experience to occur near the end of the world. In Revelation it is called the great tribulation, or the great time of testing.

2. What does this rider carry in his hand?

   "So I looked, and behold, a black horse, and he who sat on it had a pair of scales in his hand." Revelation 6:5.

This is the rider that does not utilize a weapon. **A PAIR OF SCALES** is not used to kill, but to weigh or test something. Revelation joins other Bible books that foresee a great test that is to come to all the world. This black horse and its rider foreshadows that solemn time.

When?

The Christian church has had a lot of tribulation and trial, during which the faith of believers has been severely tested, but the coming time of testing is the greatest time. Jesus described it as a time of trouble such as never was since there was a nation. There is much confusion in teachings going on today regarding when this great tribulation will take place. This need not be, for the Bible prophecies give us clear evidence of when to expect this time of trial for all. Let us examine the evidence.

3.   From what would the Philadelphians be spared?

"Because you have kept My command to persevere, I also will keep you from the hour of trial which shall come upon the whole world, to test those who dwell on the earth." Revelation 3:10.

In our study of those seven churches we learned that the Philadelphian church referred to Christianity in the 1800s. Jesus mentions to them <u>A WORLD-WIDE TEST</u> for believers was approaching, but they would not have to face it. The following church, Laodicea, must face this great time of testing, not Philadelphia.

4.   What will happen to believers after the tribulation?

"Immediately after the tribulation of those days the sun will be darkened, and the moon will not give its light; the stars will fall from heaven, and the powers of the heavens will be shaken. Then the sign of the Son of Man will appear in heaven, and then all the tribes of the earth will mourn, and they will see the Son of Man coming on the clouds of heaven with power and great glory. And He will send His angels with a great sound of a trumpet, and they will gather together His elect from the four winds, from one end of heaven to the other." Matthew 24:29-31.

Jesus tells us that the believers will be **GATHERED UP**, a reference to the rapture of believers, and this gathering up of believers will take place *<u>after</u>*, rather than *<u>before</u>*, the tribulation.

Since the tribulation will occur before the rapture of believers to heaven, this makes clear to us that we will be here to go through this great trial. This is one of the reasons Jesus gave us all this information in Revelation. He has provided the very truth we need to know to successfully navigate this treacherous time of earth's history.

5.   Before the gathering together of believers (the rapture), what must come first?

"Now, brethren, concerning the coming of our Lord Jesus Christ and our gathering together to Him, we ask you, not to be soon shaken in mind or troubled, either by spirit or by word or by letter, as if from us, as though the day of Christ had come. Let no one deceive you by any means; for that Day will not come unless the falling away comes first, and the man of sin is revealed, the son of perdition, who opposes and exalts himself above all that is called God or that is worshiped, so that he sits as God in the temple of God, showing himself that he is God." II Thessalonians 2:1-4.

Here is another Scripture that places the **FALLING AWAY** as preceding the "gathering" of believers to Christ.

The Troublemakers

Since these Scriptures make it clear that we believers will be here on earth during this time of tribulation, it is vitally important for us to study this matter carefully, so that we can be prepared. The details that will shed light on this are contained in Chapters 12-14, which elaborate on the black horse of the fourth seal.

Once again we will see that the subject material explaining each seal is found later in Revelation in the same order as the seals themselves.

Seal	Explanation
1 – White Horse	Chapter 7
2 – Red Horse	Chapters 8-11
3 – Black Horse	Chapters 12-14

As we study these chapters we will find some detailed background material leading up to the great test for all mankind, as well as a fascinating picture of the troublemakers themselves. They are three in number, and each are represented as animals. Beginning with this lesson we will look closely at the first one.

Culprit No. 1

6.   Where did this animal begin his career of troublemaking?

> *"And another sign appeared in heaven: behold, a great, fiery red dragon having seven heads and ten horns, and seven diadems on his heads." Revelation 12:3.*

The first troublemaker to be mentioned is this red dragon, and when he first appears in the vision he is pictured as **IN HEAVEN**, yet he does not remain there.

7.   Why did he leave heaven?

> *"And war broke out in heaven: Michael and his angels fought with the dragon; and the dragon and his angels fought, but they did not prevail, nor was a place found for them in heaven any longer. So the great dragon was cast out, that serpent of old, called the Devil and Satan, who deceives the whole world; he was cast to the earth, and his angels were cast out with him." Revelation 12:7-9.*

He plainly did not leave voluntarily. **HE WAS CAST OUT**. It was an exit forced upon him. How did this dragon get into heaven in the first place? What was he fighting for? The book of Revelation assumes its readers already know these details given in the Old Testament. We will now survey some of those Scriptures to understand the background of this great troublemaker for God's people.

8.   How did this heavenly creature come into being?

> *"Son of man, take up a lamentation for the king of Tyre, and say to him, Thus says the Lord God: You were the seal of perfection, full of wisdom and perfect in beauty. You were in Eden, the garden of God; every precious stone was your covering: the sardius,*

> *topaz, and diamond, beryl, onyx and jasper, sapphire, turquoise, and emerald with gold. The workmanship of your timbrels and pipes was prepared for you on the day you were created." Ezekiel 28:12, 13.*

He was not "born," **HE WAS CREATED**. He was never a baby who grew up. Adam and Eve had the same type of beginning. Although the prophecy mentions him as "the king of Tyre," we quickly see that someone else was actually intended. This individual described came into existence by a creative act, as was Adam and Eve, not by a birth. Also, he is described as once having been in the garden of Eden, a clear reference to the devil who is referred to in Revelation as "that serpent of old." Revelation 12:9.

9. What type of creature was he created to be?

> *"You were the anointed cherub who covers; I established you; you were on the holy mountain of God; you walked back and forth in the midst of fiery stones. You were perfect in your ways from the day you were created, till iniquity was found in you." Ezekiel 28:14, 15.*

This creature was once **A PERFECT CHERUB**. The fact that he is symbolized in the book of Revelation as a "dragon" does not mean that it is literally so. The Bible tells us that he is a mighty angel, created perfect and extremely beautiful. In another Scripture his name is given as "Lucifer." See Isaiah 14:12-15.

10. Who corrupted and defiled this perfect angel?

> *"Your heart was lifted up because of your beauty; you corrupted your wisdom for the sake of your splendor; I cast you to the ground, I laid you before kings, that they might gaze at you. You defiled your sanctuary by the multitude of your iniquities, by the iniquity of your trading; therefore I brought fire from your midst; it devoured you, and I turned you to ashes upon the earth in the sight of all who saw you." Ezekiel 28:17, 18.*

HE HIMSELF ruined his life with God. God never made a devil. He made a perfect angel, but that angel made a devil out of himself.

11.   What will God eventually do to him?

> *"By the abundance of your trading you became filled with violence within, and you sinned; therefore I cast you as a profane thing out of the mountain of God; and I destroyed you, O covering cherub, from the midst of the fiery stones."* Ezekiel 28:16.

The destiny of this rebellious angel is fixed by God. He said that He will **DESTROY HIM**. Just when and how God will do this will be revealed to us in the book of Revelation.

12.   How many other angels sided with him?

> *"His tail drew a third of the stars of heaven and threw them to the earth."* Revelation 12:4.

A THIRD OF THE ANGELS sided with him. He must have had a very wide influence in heaven to command such a following in his rebellion against God. While this must be an immense number, not all the angelic host joined forces with Lucifer.

13.   How successful was he with our world?

> *"So the great dragon was cast out, that serpent of old, called the Devil and Satan, who deceives the whole world . . ."* Revelation 12:9.

In just one day **THE WHOLE WORLD** joined his ranks. His success with Adam and Eve was all he needed. The laws of heredity were now working in his favor, and he gained control over all future generations.

This angel started his career of troublemaking in heaven, winning over only a third of heaven's angels. Since being cast out onto our planet he has not ceased his troublemaking. Revelation will trace his career of trouble down through the ages, climaxing with a revelation of how he will be one of the main actors in the great time of tribulation.

14. **When did this dragon attempt to destroy the special "male child?"**

> *"His tail drew a third of the stars of heaven and threw them to the earth. And the dragon stood before the woman who was ready to give birth, to devour her Child as soon as it was born. She bore a male Child who was to rule all nations with a rod of iron. And her Child was caught up to God and His throne." Revelation 12:4, 5.*

Satan's attempt to destroy Christ was immediate, **AS SOON AS HE WAS BORN.** Satan did not personally attempt this murder, but he used an agent, which from now on is represented by the dragon.

15. **Who attempted to do the dirty work for Satan?**

> *"Then Herod, when he saw that he was deceived by the wise men, was exceedingly angry; and he sent forth and put to death all the male children who were in Bethlehem and in all its districts, from two years old and under, according to the time which he had determined from the wise men." Matthew 2:16.*

HEROD, a Roman government official, sent Roman soldiers to Bethlehem. They killed all the male children, but Jesus' parents had already taken Him to Egypt. During Jesus' brief lifetime, He had no confrontation with the Roman government until Jewish leaders turned him over to them, who crucified Him.

The Roman government became the "hit man" for Satan in his efforts to destroy Jesus. Ever since, Satan has used this government to perpetrate trouble for God's people.

16. **Who next drew the wrath of this dragon?**

> *"Now when the dragon saw that he had been cast to the earth, he persecuted the woman who gave birth to the male Child." Revelation 12:13.*

THE WOMAN is the devil's next victim. In the Bible a woman is used to symbolize God's people. In the Old Testament she was spoken of as "the daughter of Zion" and in the New Testament as "the bride of Christ." The Jews were God's people at the time of Christ's birth. It is evident that this woman of Revelation was not Jesus' mother, Mary, for there is no record that she was victimized by the Roman government. Because of the rejection of Jesus by the Jewish church, Jesus set up another entity He called "His church," and it was this new Christian entity that caught the attention of this dragon.

For several centuries, the budding young movement known as Christianity, suffered greatly at the hand of this Roman dragon.

17. Where did the woman flee, to escape the next attack of this dragon?

> *"But the woman was given two wings of a great eagle, that she might fly into the wilderness to her place, where she is nourished for a time and times and half a time, from the presence of the serpent. So the serpent spewed water out of his mouth like a flood after the woman, that he might cause her to be carried away by the flood. But the earth helped the woman, and the earth opened its mouth and swallowed up the flood which the dragon had spewed out of his mouth." Revelation 12:14-16.*

The dragon followed her into **THE WILDERNESS** and there continued his pursuit of Christian believers. This particular dragon attack was of long duration. A specific time period is mentioned here. It is taken from the prophecies of Daniel and referred to several other places in the book of Revelation. We will examine this time prophecy in our next lesson and learn that it covers a span of more than 1,000 years, generally covering the time in history we call the Middle Ages. Even after this long, protracted persecution by the dragon, he does not give up.

18.   With whom does the dragon next make war?

> *"And the dragon was enraged with the woman, and he went to make war with the rest of her off-spring, who keep the commandments of God and have the testimony of Jesus Christ."* Revelation 12:17.

THE REST OF HER OFFSPRING are the next in line to receive the ire of this great troublemaker. The word "rest," in Greek, means "remaining ones," or "remnant." It is a biblical term for the Christians at the end of time. That's you and me! Satan is at war with us, and the next chapter uncovers the new agents Satan will use to try to defeat us. To be forewarned is to be forearmed!

QUIZ FOR LESSON NO. 7

Choose the correct answer:

1. What does the black horse rider use to do his work?
   (A) Bow
   (B) Sword
   (C) Scales

2. When will the tribulation occur?
   (A) Before the rapture
   (B) During the rapture
   (C) After the rapture

3. What kind of being is the Devil?
   (A) Animal
   (B) Human being
   (C) Angel

4. Who did the dragon use to attempt to murder the infant Jesus?
   (A) Himself
   (B) The Roman government
   (C) One of the angels loyal to him

5. With whom will the dragon make war in the time of the end?
   (A) The woman's man child
   (B) The woman herself
   (C) The last children of the woman

A Troublemaker of the Great Tribulation
Lesson No. 8

Culprit No. 2 (in Revelation)

In our previous lesson we learned that Revelation will portray three troublemakers who will cause the great tribulation of the future. We have already looked at the first one, and now we will notice the second one. This second one will be the main troublemaker, and is pictured not only in Revelation but also in the prophecies of Daniel. We will first look at Revelation's description, then turn to that of Daniel.

1. What did John see rising out of the sea?

   "Then I stood on the sand of the sea. And I saw a beast rising up out of the sea, having seven heads and ten horns, and on his horns ten crowns, and on his heads a blasphemous name." Revelation 13:1.

John sees emerging from the sea **A BEAST WITH SEVEN HEADS AND TEN HORNS.** This is the second agent to become a main actor in the great tribulation of the last days. It is not the same as the dragon of Chapter 12, but a different entity which definitely involves the dragon.

2. What animals are a part of this beast?

   "Now the beast which I saw was like a leopard, his feet were like the feet of a bear, and his mouth like the mouth of a lion. The dragon gave him his power, his throne, and great authority." Revelation 13:2.

This is not a literal animal, but a composite of four different animals. It looked like a **LEOPARD**, had the feet of a **BEAR** and the mouth of a **LION**. Most notable of all, the **DRAGON** that was mentioned in the previous chapter, empowered it.

These very same animals are used in a prophecy found in the book of Daniel. We will review the prophecy and learn that it identifies the same entity Revelation reveals as being a main source of trouble for God's people in the end-time. The relationship between the dragon and this new beast, which we shall hereafter refer to as the leopard-like beast, must not be quickly passed by. It will be the key to understanding just what this second beast symbolizes.

3.   **What did this beast receive from the dragon?**

"The dragon gave him his power, his throne, and great authority." Revelation 13:2.

The leopard-like beast received the **DRAGON'S THRONE** from him as a gift. We found that the dragon represents the Roman Empire. Its "throne" would be its capital seat of government, which was the city of Rome. Here is a truly amazing phenomenon! No other nation in all history actually *gave away* its capital city. Many nations have had their capital city *taken away* or destroyed, but except in the case of the Roman Empire, never has any power willingly given to another government its capital seat.

How did this come about? In the Vatican today one can view a huge 75-foot long painting. It shows Pope Sylvester receiving a figurine of a warrior from Emperor Constantine, who had built a new capital city he named Constantinople in Greece. The emperor was preparing to leave Rome permanently. Under the painting are the words: "Donation of Rome from Constantine to the Pope."

The Roman Empire gave the early Christian church leaders not only the city of Rome, but also great power and authority --- so much authority that the church eventually entered the field of politics and took over the entire empire. "Out of the ruins of political Rome arose the great moral Empire in the 'giant form' of the Roman Church." A. C. Flick, *The Rise of the Mediaeval Church (1900), p. 150.*

This is why it is still known as "the Roman Catholic Church." For many centuries it was the dominant and only Christian entity and, in these modern times, is still extremely influential in the affairs of the nations.

4.   How long would this authority last?

> *"So they worshiped the dragon who gave authority to the beast; and they worshiped the beast, saying, Who is like the beast? Who is able to make war with him? And he was given a mouth speaking great things and blasphemies, and he was given authority to continue for forty-two months." Revelation 13:4, 5.*

We are given a specific amount of time: **42 MONTHS**. This time period is mentioned seven times in the Bible, using three different terminologies:
    "1260 days" --- Revelation 11:3; 12:6.
    "42 months" --- Revelation 11:2; 13:5.
    "3 ½ times (years) --- Daniel 7:25; 12:7; Revelation 12:14.
In prophecy (see Ezekiel 4:6) a day is the symbol for a literal year, making this period 1260 years long. This was no fly-by-night, run-of-the-mill Christian organization. It was powerful for many centuries, and it is still powerful today.

5.   What would happen to this beast at the end of the 1260 years?

> *"He who leads into captivity shall go into captivity; he who kills with the sword must be killed with the sword. Here is the patience and the faith of the saints." Revelation 13:10.*

This long period of domination would come to an abrupt halt. This beast is described as suffering **CAPTIVITY** and being **KILLED WITH THE SWORD**. This is the "mortal wound" referred to earlier (verse 3). The beast would not die, as was expected, but would experience a miraculous return to power and influence.

History provides us with the details of this devastating blow. In 1798, Napoleon, the French General, dominated Europe. A French army appeared around the Vatican one day and demanded that the Pope surrender to them. Such aggressiveness by political nations toward the Papacy was unheard of for 1260 years. The Pope complied and was taken off into captivity in Southern France, where he died in exile. Two hundred years before this, the Reformation movement of Protestantism challenged the authority of the Pope, but was never able to destroy his political power as did this French military action. Ever since, the Papacy has been just one among many Christian denominations, without the political and spiritual power over people it once enjoyed. But all of this is predicted to change.

6. **With whom will this second beast make war when it achieves global power?**

"It was granted to him to make war with the saints and to overcome them. And authority was given him over every tribe, tongue, and nation. All who dwell on the earth will worship him, whose names have not been written in the Book of Life of the Lamb slain from the foundation of the world." Revelation 13:7, 8.

Here is once again pictured a resurgence of the leopard-like beast's influence and power over the world's political nations and, when it achieves its once-lost power, it will make war with **THE SAINTS**. It was a source of persecution and tribulation for 1260 long years, and it will once again direct its ire against the saints who will not worship it, resulting in a time of tribulation such as never was since there was a nation.

But before this development, there must be a revitalization of this beast. A third beast will join this second beast in causing the time of great tribulation. We will study about it in our next lesson.

Culprit No. 2 (in Daniel)

In the Old Testament, the Lord showed the prophet Daniel the very same entity, using different symbolism.

7. **What four animals came up from the sea?**

"Daniel spoke, saying, I saw in my visions by night, and behold, the four winds of heaven were stirring up the Great Sea. And four great beasts came up from the sea, each different from the other. The first was like a lion, and had eagle's wings. I watched till its wings were plucked off; and it was lifted up from the earth and made to stand on two feet like a man, and a man's heart was given to it. And suddenly another beast, a second, like a bear. It was

raised up on one side, and had three ribs in its mouth between its teeth. And they said thus to it: Arise, devour much flesh! After this I looked, and there was another, like a leopard, which had on its back four wings of a bird. The beast also had four heads and dominion was given to it. After this I saw in the night visions, and behold, a fourth beast, dreadful and terrible, exceedingly strong. It had huge iron teeth; it was devouring, breaking in pieces, and trampling the residue with its feet. It was different from all the beasts that were before it, and it had ten horns." Daniel 7:2-7.

From our study in Revelation, these animals are familiar to us. First there was a **LION**; then a **BEAR**; then a **LEOPARD**. The fourth animal, the **DRAGON**, is important to us, because we have met him before, in Revelation 12.

8.   What did each of these animals represent?

"Those great beasts, which are four, are four kings which arise out of the earth." Daniel 7:17.

It was explained to Daniel that these animals represented **FOUR KINGDOMS WHICH WILL ARISE**. The first three are identified earlier in Daniel's book. The lion was Babylon; the bear was Medo-Persia; and the leopard was Greece.

9.   What did the fourth animal represent?

"Thus he said: The fourth beast shall be a fourth kingdom on earth, which shall be different from all other kingdoms, and shall devour the whole earth, trample it and break it in pieces." Daniel 7:23.

This beast represented **A FOURTH KINGDOM**. The fourth (the dragon) was not named, because it had not yet come into existence in Daniel's time. History us clearly tells us that it was the Roman Empire that wrestled world domination from Greece and became the lone super power of its day.

10. What do the ten horns represent?

> "The ten horns are ten kings who shall arise from this kingdom. And another shall rise after them. He shall be different from the first ones, and shall subdue three kings." Daniel 7:24.

Since the dragon-like beast represents the Roman Empire, the ten horns growing out of it would naturally represent **TEN NATIONS THAT EMERGE FROM ROME**. The Roman Empire disintegrated into separate nations which are now the modern European nations. Three of the ten are now extinct.

11. What else grew out of this Roman dragon?

> "I was considering the horns, and there was another horn, a little one, coming up among them, before whom three of the first horns were plucked out by the roots. And there, in this horn, were eyes like the eyes of a man, and a mouth speaking pompous words." Daniel 7:8.

After ten horns emerged, **ANOTHER LITTLE HORN** is produced by this Roman dragon. In this vision the eleventh horn is described in detail. It is this symbolic horn that is described with the exact same characteristics of the leopard-like beast in Revelation 13.

12. Matching the description of the little horn in Daniel with the leopard-like beast in Revelation, it is apparent that they are one and the same entity, though differently symbolized.

> "He shall speak pompous words against the Most High, shall persecute the saints of the Most High, and shall intend to change times and law. Then the saints shall be given into his hand for a time and times and half a time." Daniel 7:25.

In Daniel, he shall "speak pompous words against the Most High;" in Revelation, he shall "**SPEAK GREAT THINGS AND BLASPHEMIES**." In Daniel, he will "persecute the saints of the Most High;" in Revelation, he will "**MAKE WAR WITH THE SAINTS**." In Daniel, "the saints shall be given into his hand;" in Revelation, he will "**OVERCOME THEM**." In Daniel, he will reign "for a time and times and half a time;" in Revelation, for "**42 MONTHS**."

13.   What would this little horn do to "times and law?"

"He . . . shall intend to change times and law." Daniel 7:25.

He will **INTEND TO CHANGE THEM**. There would be nothing unusual or wrong for a government to change some of its laws, but to attempt to change God's law is so serious a matter that the prophecy mentions this.

14.   What two things enrage the dragon today?

"And the dragon was enraged with the woman, and he went to make war with the rest of her off-spring, who keep the commandments of God and have the testimony of Jesus Christ." Revelation 12:17.

It is apparent that the dragon, like the leopard-like beast, will take issue with the end-time believers about **THE COMMANDMENTS OF GOD**, and **THE TESTIMONY OF JESUS CHRIST**. This controversy will break out into the great tribulation, which will be a test of the faith of all true believers. They will be joined by a third beast, and together they will be a trio of trouble. This will be the subject of our next lesson.

QUIZ FOR LESSON NO. 8

True or False:

1. The leopard-like beast gave power to the dragon to get it started.

2. The leopard-like beast came from heaven.

3. The leopard-like beast inherited its headquarters city from the Roman dragon.

4. The leopard-like beast of Revelation and the little horn of Daniel's dragon symbolize the same thing.

5. The leopard-like beast attempted to change some of God's laws.

The Lamb-like Beast
Lesson No. 9

We are studying the great tribulation, which is symbolized by the rider on that black horse. He utilizes a pair of scales with which to test all mankind, causing a time of trouble such as never was since there was a nation. In Revelation 12-14, we see a fuller picture of this tribulation, and it is caused by three main culprits. In our last lesson we looked carefully at the second culprit, the leopard-like beast. Let us briefly review what we learned about it.

Culprit No. 2

The leopard-like beast we studied in our last lesson got its start from the Roman dragon. Once in power, the prophecy told us that the leopard-like beast was to reign for 1260 years, terminating with a "mortal wound" that would be healed, bringing it into world-wide prominence once again.

1. What would happen to one of its heads?

   "And I saw one of his heads as if it had been mortally wounded, and his deadly wound was healed. And all the world marveled and followed the beast." Revelation 13:3.

John notices that one of its heads had been **MORTALLY WOUNDED**. This seemed to be a "mortal wound" that would terminate its life, but the prophecy says it would survive and be healed.

2. Where would this beast end up when it would be "killed with the sword?"

   "He who leads into captivity shall go into captivity." Revelation 13:10.

It would not end up in the grave, but **IN CAPTIVITY**. This beast's world supremacy would not be terminated by death, but by captivity. In 1798, an atheistic French army was sent to Rome to challenge the Papacy. The Pope surrendered and was taken captive to France, ending the Papacy's political career for the first time in 1260 years.

3.   What would happen to this "deadly wound?"

> "... and his deadly wound was healed. And all the world marveled and followed the beast." Revelation 13:3.

Its deadly wound would be **HEALED**. This indicates that its sovereignty and supremacy among nations would be restored. In 1929, the Lateran Treaty, negotiated with Mussolini, the ruler of Italy at the time, restored to the Papacy sovereign authority over what is now called Vatican City. With this arrangement it became a sovereign government, independent of Italy. This is why today the Vatican exchanges ambassadors with other nations, just as all sovereign nations do. Churches do not have this feature about them. However, the world recognizes that the Papacy is more than a church. It is a political entity that is becoming more and more respected in political circles.

Culprit No. 3

4.   What animal next appears in John's vision?

> "Then I saw another beast coming up out of the earth, and he had two horns like a lamb and spoke like a dragon." Revelation 13:11.

A LAMB-LIKE BEAST appears on the scene. This is the third animal that will participate in the troubles of God's people during the great tribulation. It will be this animal that will lead the way in bringing the leopard-like beast to international power and influence.

Notice that the dragon will influence this beast also, as it did the leopard-like beast.

5.   From where did this animal originate?

"Then I saw another beast coming up out of the earth . . ." Revelation 13:11.

It does not emerge from the sea, as did the leopard-like beast of Revelation or the four beasts of Daniel's vision. It arose **OUT OF THE EARTH**. This is one of many clues that help us identify the new world power that comes on the scene in the last days.

[1] It appears on the scene at the time of captivity of the leopard-like beast in 1798 (verse 10).

[2] The leopard-like beast, as well as the four beasts of Daniel 7, emerged from the sea. But this beast emerged from the "earth," a term indicating a relatively unpopulated area (verse 11). In other words, it did not conquer another nation in order to get established.

[3] It is not a wild beast that has war-like tendencies, but it is likened to a docile lamb (verse 11).

[4] It would be a superpower, with ability to influence the entire world (verse 12).

The only nation rising to become such a superpower at this specific time is the United States of America. No other power fits all of these specifications.

6. **What will this new beast cause the world to do?**

"And he exercises all the authority of the first beast in his presence, and causes the earth and those who dwell in it to worship the first beast, whose deadly wound was healed." Revelation 13:12.

This new beast does not pursue an agenda of its own, but urges all **TO WORSHIP THE LEOPARD-LIKE BEAST.** While it has a lamb-like appearance, it will eventually influence the world to acquiesce to the worship demanded by the leopard-like beast. These two entities will be in perfect agreement with each other. Together they will set the stage for "the hour of trial which shall come upon the whole world, to test those who dwell on the earth . . ." Revelation 3:10.

The Tribulation Arrives

7.   What special entity is created?

"And he deceives those who dwell on the earth by those signs which he was granted to do in the sight of the beast, telling those who dwell on the earth to make an image to the beast who was wounded by the sword and lived." Revelation 13:14.

This prophecy goes on to explain just how the lamb-like beast will support and promote the agenda of the leopard-like beast. It will begin by "telling those who dwell on the earth" to make **AN IMAGE TO THE LEOPARD-LIKE BEAST**. Remember that this nation arose from "the earth" (verse 11). Therefore, "those who dwell on the earth" would be a reference to its own citizens.

The nation of America is a political entity that has written in its Constitution that congress shall make no law regarding religion, or the free exercise thereof. Yet this prophecy says that it will reverse that long-held principle and enter the field of religion.

An image is something very similar. While the Papacy (the leopard-like beast) combines both religious and political authority, so the United States government will be altered to create a similar organization with Protestantism, and its goals will be identical to those of the Papacy.

8.   What will everyone be required to receive?

"He causes all, both small and great, rich and poor, free and slave, to receive a mark on their right hand or on their foreheads." Revelation 13:16.

A MARK will be imposed on all, to show compliance. How is this mark administered? The text says that "He causes" it to be received. How does a government usually obtain compliance? Certainly not by asking for volunteer compliance, or by mere pleading, but by making laws. Governments have authority to control its citizens by legislation, and with it will come penalties for non-compliance.

This test will not only be personal, but universal. All will be involved, and no one will be able to stay neutral.

9. What will people be prohibited from doing if they refuse this mark?

"And that no one may buy or sell except one who has the mark or the name of the beast, or the number of his name." Revelation 13:17.

There will be an initial penalty attached to the law. The ability of non-conformers to **BUY OR SELL** will be removed. Until these modern times, never in the history of nations has there been the possibility for a government having the power to control the buying and selling of its citizens. Our modern society is now computer driven and credit-card oriented. This has produced the possibility of changing to a cashless society. The advantages of convenience and security are so great, that this could now become a viable possibility. But with these advantages comes a grave danger. Whatever entity gains full control of computerized transactions can control its usage. The most logical and natural result will be for the government to be the controlling watch dog and enforcer of "proper usage" of this technology. In this way, the governments of the world can control the ability of all its citizens to "buy or sell."

There are always possibilities to circumvent and avoid compliance to human laws. Closing loopholes and instituting stiffer penalties is always the reaction.

10. What will be the final penalty for refusing this mark?

> *"He was granted power to give breath to the image of the beast, that the image of the beast should both speak and cause as many as would not worship the image of the beast to be killed." Revelation 13:15.*

Believers will be severely put to the test when this happens. The adding of a **DEATH PENALTY** to the controversial law will truly bring to reality the symbolism of that black horse and its rider wielding a pair of scales.

Chapter 13 unveils how Satan will use governmental laws to remove religious freedom and pressure everyone to accept and obey the demands of his agents. Jesus referred to this time as "great tribulation, such as has not been since the beginning of the world until this time, no, nor ever shall be." Matthew 24:21. But God will not sit idly by in all of this. Chapter 14 unveils how God will act to help us through this very difficult time.

God's Solution

11. What will be the final penalty for accepting this mark?

> *"Then a third angel followed them, saying with a loud voice, If anyone worships the beast and his image, and receives his mark on his forehead or on his hand, he himself shall also drink of the wine of the wrath of God, which is poured out full strength into the cup of His indignation. He shall be tormented with fire and brimstone in the presence of the holy angels and in the presence of the Lamb." Revelation 14:9,10.*

Many will be led to feel that they will be free of danger if they yield to the beast and accept its mark. Those who surrender to the demands of human laws, thinking they will save their lives, will discover that their decision will bring down upon them an even worse penalty from God. This angel sent from God warns of a dreadful, two-fold punishment. They will **[1] DRINK OF THE WRATH OF GOD** (this is the seven last plagues mentioned in the next two chapters of Revelation), and will be **[2] TORMENTED WITH FIRE AND BRIMSTONE** (described fully in future chapters of Revelation).

12. **How are those described who refuse the mark?**

   "Here is the patience of the saints; here are those who keep the commandments of God and the faith of Jesus." Revelation 14:12.

This is said only of those who resist this mark that is universally imposed. They **KEEP GOD'S COMMANDMENTS** and **HAVE FAITH IN JESUS**.

Revelation warns of a future "mark" that must be refused if we are to be saved. It does not, however, give any details about that mark so that we can recognize it and refuse it. The reason is that we do not need this information in order to avoid getting the mark. It clearly shows that those who do not have the mark are those who keep God's commandments and are loyal to Jesus. Anyone who receives the mark must accept what the beast and its image says, over what Jesus and God's commandments require.

The commandments of God will be at the core of the issue at that time. There will evidently be a clear difference between God's commandments and what the beast and its image are aggressively advocating.

13. **If we accept religious traditions over the commandments of God, how did Jesus say that would affect our worship of Him?**

   "He answered and said to them, Well did Isaiah prophesy of you hypocrites, as it is written: This people honors Me with their lips, but their heart is far from Me, and in vain they worship Me, teaching as doctrines the commandments of men. For laying aside the commandment of God, you hold the tradition of men --- the washing of pitchers and cups, and many other such things you do. He said to them, All too well you reject the commandment of God, that you may keep your tradition." Mark 7:6-9.

Satan manipulated the Jews of old to develop religious practices that would cause people to disregard God's commandments. Satan will use the same tactic in the last days, and all will have to decide whether to follow man or God.

The Jews in Jesus' day faced the same test. Their leaders were urging that all worship God in the way their traditions dictated. But because those ways of worshiping God cut directly across God's commandments, Jesus asserted that their worship of God was **IN VAIN**.

Today it is not Jewish religious traditions, but Christian religious traditions that are urged upon us, in spite of the fact that these man-made traditions force us to blatantly disobey God's Ten Commandments. It is easy to pick out these problem practices in today's popular religion.

14. What will the "little horn" of Daniel's vision attempt to do to God's laws?

"And [the little horn] shall intend to change times and laws." Daniel 7:25.

These laws spoken of here must be God's law, not man's, since the previous verse says that "He shall speak pompous words against the Most High." It would be indeed a pompous act to **CHANGE THEM**, since that would be putting man above God, Who originated them. Yet that is precisely what has been attempted by Christian leaders.

15. What does God's second commandment tell us not to use in our worship?

"You shall not make for yourself a carved image --- any likeness of anything that is in heaven above, or that is in the earth beneath, or that is in the water under the earth; you shall not bow down to them nor serve them. For I the Lord your God, am a jealous God, visiting the iniquity of the fathers upon the children to the third and fourth generations of those who hate Me, but showing mercy to thousands, to those who love Me and keep My commandments." Exodus 20:4-6.

The first commandment forbids worshiping other gods. The second commandment forbids use of **IMAGES** in our worship of God Himself. Catholic catechisms eliminate this commandment altogether in their list of God's Ten Commandments, splitting the last commandment into two parts to maintain the number ten.

The reason for this tampering with God's commandments is to justify their centuries-old tradition of utilizing images in their worship of God.

16. What day of the week does God's fourth commandment identify as the day of worship?

"Remember the Sabbath day, to keep it holy. Six days you shall labor and do all your work, but the seventh day is the Sabbath of

the Lord your God. In it you shall do no work: you, nor your son, nor your daughter, nor your male servant, nor your female servant, nor your cattle, nor your stranger who is within your gates. For in six days the Lord made the heavens and the earth, the sea, and all that is in them, and rested the seventh day. Therefore the Lord blessed the Sabbath day and hallowed it." Exodus 20:8-11.

God goes to great length to identify **THE SEVENTH DAY** that He has made holy, and commands us to honor Him by keeping it holy. In spite of this great emphasis on the part of God to point out one particular day, almost all Christendom today has set aside this explicit command of God and set up a different day of worship. This radical change of God's law was instituted many centuries ago when there was only one Christian organization in existence, and they freely admit this.

"Q. Which is the Sabbath day?
A. Saturday is the Sabbath day.
Q. Why do we observe Sunday instead of Saturday?
A. We observe Sunday instead of Saturday, because the Catholic Church transferred the solemnity from Saturday to Sunday."
The Convert's Catechism of Catholic Doctrine (1957 ed.) p. 50.

This attempt to make such drastic changes to God's Ten Commandments was not done out of any hostility toward God. They were made in good faith, believing that Jesus granted the right to future Christian leaders to make such changes.

Ironically, in spite of their insistence on following the Bible rather than church traditions, Protestants agree wholeheartedly on this religious practice. Thus they are set to enter into a partnership one day to enforce this strange method of worship over that dictated by the commandments of God. When that occurs, the issue will be over how we worship God, and the Ten Commandments will be at the very heart of the controversy. It will put everyone to the test whether God's commandments or the beast's traditions will be personally adopted.

For many the results will be announced by God: "You have been weighed in the balances, and found wanting." Daniel 5:27.

QUIZ FOR LESSON NO. 9

A. RED DRAGON
B. LEOPARD-LIKE BEAST
C. LAMB-LIKE BEAST

1. This animal gives help and support to the leopard-like beast.

2. This animal emerged out of the sea.

3. This animal emerged out of the earth.

4. This animal puts a mark on those who obey it.

5. The lamb-like animal will someday speak like this animal.

Weighed In the Balances
Lesson No. 10

The Black Horse

We are still studying the details Revelation gives which will open to us the significance of the third seal featuring a black horse and its rider.

1. What device did the black horse rider hold?

    "When He opened the third seal, I heard the third living creature say, Come and see. So I looked, and behold, a black horse, and he who sat on it had a pair of scales in his hand." Revelation 6:5.

A PAIR OF SCALES is not used as a weapon, but as an instrument to weigh, or test something. This is the only horse rider with no weapon, but the horse is nonetheless extremely important.

2. What is the basic purpose of God allowing this time of tribulation?

    "Because you have kept My command to persevere, I also will keep you from the hour of trial which shall come upon the whole world, to test those who dwell on the earth." Revelation 3:10.

The purpose of **A TEST** is not to torment, but to reveal. This is why a test is often called an "examination." It reveals to the tester what we know and also reveals to us, the tested, things we did not realize about ourselves.

Tribulation troubles are orchestrated by the devil dragon and his special agents, but God is also interested in the results.

The Tester

3. Whom did the Psalmist ask to examine him?

    "Search me, O God, and know my heart; try me, and know my anxieties." Psalm 139:23.

GOD is in the testing business, but not for the same reasons Satan is. Satan's ultimate goal is to intimidate us into disobeying God, using hardships and even the threat of death. However, God's goal in testing us is to open our eyes to things we need to understand in order to be saved.

4.   What are the two goals God has for testing us?

"And see if there is any wicked way in me, and lead me in the way everlasting." Psalm 139:24.

God has worthy goals in mind. He puts us to the test **[1] TO REVEAL ANY WICKED WAY IN US** and **[2] TO LEAD US IN THE RIGHT WAY**. This is what is going on in our walk with God today. We are daily being tested by God. As we submit and allow Him to change the wrong things in our lives, we are preparing for the final exam that will come to everyone some day.

Neither God nor Satan is waiting for the great time of testing that will come to all the world. They are both working in advance to prepare people for that global crisis, and our reactions in that final test will reflect our present decisions.

The Testing Instrument

5. God gave bread from heaven to the Israelites to test their willingness to do what?

"Then the Lord said to Moses, Behold, I will rain bread from heaven for you. And the people shall go out and gather a certain quota every day, that I may test them, whether they will walk in My law or not. And it shall be on the sixth day that they shall prepare what they bring in, and it shall be twice as much as they gather daily." Exodus 16:4, 5.

This was to be a test of their willingness TO **WALK IN GOD'S LAW**. It was not a difficult test requiring exceptional brain power. It was a simple command. The test God gave Adam and Eve was also very simple. At that time He used a tree. Let us watch what God used with the Israelites to test their willingness to believe and obey God.

6.   On what day were they not to gather bread?

"And so it was, on the sixth day, that they gathered twice as much bread, two omers for each one. And all the rulers of the congre-

gation came and told Moses. Then he said to them, This is what the Lord has said: Tomorrow is a Sabbath rest, a holy Sabbath to the Lord. Bake what you will bake today, and boil what you will boil; and lay up for yourselves all that remains, to be kept until morning. So they laid it up till morning, as Moses commanded; and it did not stink, nor were there any worms in it. Then Moses said, Eat that today, for today is a Sabbath to the Lord; today you will not find it in the field. Six days you shall gather it, but on the seventh day, the Sabbath, there will be none." Exodus 16:22-26.

God used **THE SEVENTH-DAY SABBATH** of His Ten Commandments to test their obedience.

7. **What were the people refusing to do by going out to hunt for bread on the Sabbath day?**

"Then it happened that some of the people went out on the seventh day to gather, but they found none. And the Lord said to Moses, How long do you refuse to keep My commandments and My laws? See! For the Lord has given you the Sabbath; therefore He gives you on the sixth day bread for two days. Let every man remain in his place; let no man go out of his place on the seventh day. So the people rested on the seventh day." Exodus 16:27-30.

When God tests individuals He usually asks them to do something simple to reveal their faith in Him. In this case, by refusing **TO OBEY GOD'S COMMANDMENTS** they were revealing their lack of faith in God.

8. **What specific day does the fourth commandment point to as the Sabbath?**

"Remember the Sabbath day, to keep it holy. Six days you shall labor and do all your work, but the seventh day is the Sabbath of the Lord your God. In it you shall do no work: you, nor your son, nor your daughter, nor your male servant, nor your female servant, nor your cattle, nor your stranger who is within your gates. For in six days the Lord made the heavens and the earth, the sea, and all that is in them, and rested the seventh day. Therefore the Lord blessed the Sabbath day and hallowed it." Exodus 20:8-11.

God Himself has set aside as holy, a specific special day. He states that it is **THE SEVENTH DAY**. He wrote it in stone to make it as clear as possible for all. In the past He used it as a testing instrument for His people, and they finally learned their lesson. They became ardent Sabbath keepers. This was a very important matter to God. In Exodus 31:13, He established Sabbath keeping as a sign that they were God's special people: "Speak also to the children of Israel, saying: Surely My Sabbaths you shall keep, for it is a sign between Me and you throughout your generations, that you may know that I am the Lord who sanctifies you."

In these closing days of earth's history, God will utilize the same testing instrument which will discern "Between the righteous and the wicked, between one who serves God and one who does not serve Him," Malachi 3:18.

The traditional symbol of justice is a blindfolded woman holding a scale. The scale has two sides. One side is for the individual under investigation, and the other is for the law. The "woman" doesn't decide, because she is blindfolded. The law is the final authority. God gave the Israelites His commandment to regard the seventh day as a holy day. When their works did not match what God commanded, they failed His test of obedience in spite of any insistence from them that they still loved Him.

The Commandment Test

9. **In the last days, what do the true followers of Jesus do that provokes Satan?**

    "And the dragon was enraged with the woman, and he went to make war with the rest of her offspring, who keep the commandments of God and have the testimony of Jesus." Revelation 12:17.

There are many who profess loyalty to Jesus in the last days, but when Satan sees that they also **KEEP GOD'S COMMANDMENTS**, he is fully aroused to wage war against them.

10. **How does Revelation describe those who maintain their faith in Jesus during these days?**
    "Here is the patience of the saints; here are those who keep the commandments of God and the faith of Jesus." Revelation 14:12.

Once again we see this combination of faith and commandments, describing God's people in the time of the end. That these are Christians is evidenced by the fact that they are loyal to Jesus. At the same time, they **KEEP GOD'S COMMANDMENTS**.

Since God's faithful people in the time of the end will be commandment keepers, they will be keepers of the seventh-day Sabbath, because that is one of God's commands. In fact, it is the longest, most detailed of all the ten! Evidently this issue is a big one in the mind of God who gave those Ten Commandments.

11. How many of the Ten Commandments do we have to keep in order to qualify as commandment keepers?

> *"For whoever shall keep the whole law, and yet stumble in one point, he is guilty of all. For He who said, Do not commit adultery, also said, Do not murder. Now if you do not commit adultery, but you do murder, you have become a transgressor of the law." James 2:10, 11.*

We are not at liberty to pick and choose which commandments we will obey and which ones we will ignore. We are under obligation to keep **ALL TEN OF THEM**. Otherwise we are commandment breakers, not commandment keepers. This principle holds true in our time as it did in James' day.

12. Who will receive heaven's approval?

> *"Do not think that I came to destroy the Law or the Prophets. I did not come to destroy but to fulfill. For assuredly, I say to you, till heaven and earth pass away, one jot or one tittle will by no means pass from the law till all is fulfilled. Whoever therefore breaks one of the least of these commandments, and teaches men so, shall be called least in the kingdom of heaven; but whoever does and teaches them, he shall be called great in the kingdom of heaven." Matthew 5:17-19.*

Jesus says that **COMMANDMENT KEEPERS** are great in the estimate of heaven, and those who violate them and teach others to do so also are viewed in a very bad light in the eyes of heaven.

13. Those who will someday enter the kingdom of heaven will be doing what?

> *"Blessed are those who do His commandments, that they may have the right to the tree of life, and may enter through the gates into the city." Revelation 22:14.*

Only those who are **KEEPING GOD'S COMMANDMENTS** will have entrance into that heavenly city of the New Jerusalem. The next verse describes those who are shut out, and it is clear that they are those who violate those high and holy principles: "But outside are dogs and sorcerers and sexually immoral and murderers and idolaters, and whoever loves and practices a lie (verse 15)."

From the first to the last book, the New Testament is emphatic in its support of the Ten Commandments.

14.   What is one thing God's commandments are not?

>   *"By this we know that we love the children of God, when we love God and keep His commandments. For this is the love of God, that we keep His commandments. And His commandments are not burdensome." I John 5:2, 3.*

Those who have adopted the Ten Commandments as the guiding principles of their lives do not find them **BURDENSOME**. On the contrary, they find them a delight and the source of a happy, peaceful and meaningful relationship with God and their fellow men.

Satan is preparing the world for the great crisis that is just ahead. He too has studied Revelation, and he knows that God's Ten Commandments will be the central issue. He works to convince people that Jesus has released us from the necessity of obeying God's commandments, because they are so burdensome.

The Testimony of Others

In spite of the fact that Sunday is advocated as a Christian holy day by almost all denominations, many honest scholars have admitted that the Bible does not support it.

BAPTIST

"There was and is a commandment to keep holy the Sabbath day, but that day was not Sunday. . . . It will be said, however, and with some show of triumph, that the Sabbath was transferred from the seventh to the first day of the week. . . . Of course, I quite well know that Sunday did come into use in early Christian history as a religious day, as we learn from the

Christian Fathers and other sources. But what a pity that it comes branded with the mark of paganism, and christened with the name of the sun god." Dr. Edward T. Hiscox, author of *The Baptist Manual,* in a paper read before a New York ministers' conference held Nov. 13, 1893.

CATHOLIC

"You may read the Bible from Genesis to Revelation, and you will not find a single line authorizing the sanctification of Sunday. The Scriptures enforce the religious observance of Saturday, a day which we never sanctify." Cardinal Gibbons, *The Faith of Our Fathers (92nd ed., rev.),* p. 89.

EPISCOPAL

"Is there any command in the New Testament to change the day of weekly rest from Saturday to Sunday? None." *Manual of Christian Doctrine,* p. 127.

LUTHERAN

"They (Catholics) allege the Sabbath changed into Sunday, the Lord's Day, contrary to the Decalogue, as it appears, neither is there any example more boasted of than the changing of the Sabbath day. Great, say they, is the power and authority of the church, since it dispensed with one of the Ten Commandments." Martin Luther, *Augsburg Confession of Faith,* art. 28, par. 9.

METHODIST

"The reason we observe the first day instead of the seventh is based on no positive command. One will search the Scriptures in vain for authority for changing from the seventh day to the first. The early Christians began to worship on the first day of the week because Jesus rose from the dead on that day. By and by, this day of worship was made also a day of rest, a legal holiday. This took place in the year 321. Our Christian Sabbath, therefore, is not a matter of positive command. It is a gift of the church." Clovis G. Chappell, *Ten Rules for Living,* p. 61

PRESBYTERIAN

"The Sabbath is a part of the Decalogue --- the Ten Commandments. This alone forever settles the question as to the perpetuity of the institution. . . . Until, therefore, it can be shown that the whole moral law has been repealed, the Sabbath will stand. . . . The teaching of Christ confirms the perpetuity of the Sabbath." T. C. Blake, *Theology Condensed,* pp. 474, 475.

QUIZ FOR LESSON NO. 10

Fill In the Blank:

    SPECIAL
    SCALES
    SABBATH
    SIGN
    SEVENTH

1. Instead of a sword, the black horse rider carries S_____.

2. In the past, the testing instrument God used to test His people's loyalty was the S_____.

3. The Bible Sabbath is the S_____ day of the week.

4. Keeping God's Sabbath holy is a S___ that we put God before any man.

5. Sabbath-keeping sets us apart and makes us a S_____ people to God.

A Unique Product of God's Ingenuity
Lesson No. 11

For centuries the true Bible Sabbath has been unknown to the majority of Christians. Today, with a renewed interest in Revelation and its supportive Scriptures, an awareness of a difference between church traditions and the Bible has created a great spiritual movement of Sabbath keepers. Because of the newness of this truth to so many, it would be helpful to take a close look at this creation of God.

The inventive talent of the God of heaven is reflected in the products of the week of creation. The seventh-day Sabbath is one of those products that is very special. Here are some of the characteristics of this divine invention that indicate its uniqueness.

CREATED

1. How did Jesus say the Sabbath came into existence?

   "And He said to them, The Sabbath was made for man, and not man for the Sabbath." Mark 2:27.

Here Jesus describes just how the Sabbath came into existence: **IT WAS MADE.** The seventh day did not automatically become a Sabbath without God doing anything to it. It was an invention which He purposely brought into existence. In order for a day to be a Sabbath, it has to be *made* that way. No one can make a day holy, except God. We can accept it, or reject it, but its holiness cannot be changed or transferred by man to any other day.

THE LORD'S DAY

2. Which day of the week did Jesus claim as His special day?

   "Therefore the Son of Man is also Lord of the Sabbath." Mark 2:28.

Jesus designated **THE SABBATH** as the only day He calls "the Lord's day." Since the Lord made all the days, He alone decides which day He will honor above the others. People today are taught to believe that Sunday is the Lord's day, a day different from the Sabbath. The Bible says that the Lord's day and the Sabbath day are one and the same. It is impossible to separate Christ from the Sabbath. It is His special day.

INVISIBLE

3.   What two things did God do to that day?

> *"Thus the heavens and the earth, and all the host of them, were finished. And on the seventh day God ended His work which He had done, and He rested on the seventh day from all His work which He had done. Then God blessed the seventh day and sanctified it, because in it He rested from all His work which God created and made." Genesis 2:1-3.*

HE BLESSED AND SANCTIFIED IT. What God did to the seventh day is not observable to human eyes. All the things God made on the previous six days were things that could be physically observed. To human beings, all seven of the days appear identical; there is no visible difference. However, God insists that the seventh day is different. Therefore, for us to accept the seventh day as holy requires faith in God.

RESTRICTED

4.   Which days did God bless and hallow?

> *"For in six days the Lord made the heavens and the earth, the sea, and all that is in them, and rested the seventh day. Therefore the Lord blessed the Sabbath day and hallowed it." Exodus 20:11.*

This special thing that God did to create a Sabbath was done to **ONLY THE SEVENTH DAY**. No other options were proposed. The Sabbath was assigned to only one particular day of the week. All other created works of God share all seven of the days. Not so, the sacredness of the seventh day. It remains within the sunset boundaries of one particular day. Nothing else that God created during that creation week was restricted to only one day.

INDESTRUCTIBLE

5. Which of the seven days will be used for worship in eternity?

"For as the new heavens and the new earth which I will make shall remain before Me, says the Lord, So shall your descendants and your name remain. And it shall come to pass that from one New Moon to another, and from one Sabbath to another, all flesh shall come to worship before Me, says the Lord." Isaiah 66:22, 23.

THE SABBATH DAY is the only thing God created during creation week that will not be replaced by something new. It is the only product of God's original creation that is unaffected by sin.

FOR HUMANS ONLY

6. For whose benefit was the Sabbath made?

"And He said to them, The Sabbath was made for man, and not man for the Sabbath." Mark 2:27.

God only had **MAN** in mind, when He created this unique entity. The Sabbath is unknown and unobserved by the rest of nature. The sun shines in it, as in the other six days; plants grow and do their everyday thing on that sacred day; and animals do not acknowledge it. It was designed to be a blessing mainly for us humans.

GOD'S SIGN/SEAL

7. What does the Bible call the Sabbath?

"Hallow My Sabbaths, and they will be a sign between Me and you, that you may know that I am the Lord your God." Ezekiel 20:20.

"**SIGN**" and "seal" are used interchangeably in the Bible. See Romans 4:11. The observance of God's true Sabbath is involved with God's seal mentioned in Revelation. Interestingly, the Papacy claims that Sunday-keeping is the "sign" or "mark" of their own religious authority. The Chancellor for Cardinal Gibbons wrote on November 11, 1895: "Of course the Catholic Church claims that the change was her act. It could not have been otherwise, as no one in those days would have dreamed of doing anything in matters spiritual, and ecclesiastical, and religious, without her. And the act is a mark of her ecclesiastical authority in religious things."

I should make it clear that this act was not done out of maliciousness or sinister rebellion against God. They felt quite clear in their conscience to do this because of a very fundamental, but erroneous, point of doctrine they held. It was their understanding that since the church produced the Bible, they could make any changes to it in the future they felt would be convenient. The basic belief of Catholicism is that the Church has higher authority than the Bible, while one of the main beliefs of Protestantism is that the Bible is above the church. If there was a disagreement between the two, the church must change its tradition, "But the word of the Lord endures forever" I Peter 1:25.

It is ironical and regrettable that Protestants accept the Catholic change of an important part of God's Word, in spite of their insistence that the Bible should be accepted above any church tradition or teaching.

HOW IS THE SABBATH KEPT HOLY?

It is exciting to discover which day of the week is the true day in which God infused a special holiness. Yet, there awaits an even greater thrill as we learn how to preserve the holiness of that day by "keeping" it holy. The Scriptures provide us with clear instructions on how to do this.

SUNSET TO SUNSET

8. What is the time frame for celebration of the Sabbath?

> *"It shall be to you a Sabbath of solemn rest, and you shall afflict your souls; on the ninth day of the month at evening, from evening to evening, you shall celebrate your Sabbath." Leviticus 23:32.*

FROM EVENING TO EVENING is a biblical expression describing the boundaries of this sacred day. The Sabbath begins and ends with a sunset. At first this may seem strange to us, because today we measure our days from midnight to midnight. This custom, however, is only a modern practice. The biblical days were divided by sunsets, beginning with the first seven creation days. This is why the Sabbath must be kept holy from sunset on Friday night to sunset on Saturday night. The time between these two sunsets will be the only time of the entire week that God made holy.

This concept is affirmed by Mark 1:32 where it clearly states what the Bible means by "evening:" "At evening, when the sun had set, they brought to Him all who were sick and those who were demon-possessed."

In our modern understanding of time we "start our day" in the morning, the daylight hours. However, according to biblical reckoning of time, when we go to work in the morning our day is already half over! We can use human understanding of time for our daily life, but when it comes to keeping holy all 24 hours of the day God made holy, we must use the Bible system of reckoning, because it coincides with creation time.

REST FROM EMPLOYMENT

9. **What should we not do on the Sabbath?**

> *"But the seventh day is the Sabbath of the Lord your God. In it you shall do no work: you, nor your son, nor your daughter, nor your male servant, nor your female servant, not your cattle, nor your stranger who is within your gates." Exodus 20:10.*

One of the main elements of Sabbath-keeping is resting from our **WORK,** or employment. Making arrangements to be free from our regular employment during those sacred hours will provide us an oasis of rest and enjoyment at the end of each week.

The Bible assures us that there is some very necessary work that must be done on the Sabbath hour, and these were exceptions, rather than the rule. Jesus said that ". . . on the Sabbath the priests in the temple profane the Sabbath, and are blameless" Matthew 12:4. Jesus healed sick people on the Sabbath (Luke 14:1-5) and taught that emergencies should be cared for (Matthew 12:10-12). The commandment prohibition of "work" refers to our normal secular employment. Such employment is not wrong to engage in on the other days of the week, but become wrong if done on the Sabbath, for it violates its basic purpose to provide us with rest and relaxation, as well as provide us with time to pursue our relationship with God.

AVOID BUYING AND SELLING

10. What other activity profanes the Sabbath?

> *"In those days I saw people in Judah treading wine presses on the Sabbath, and bringing in sheaves, and loading donkeys with wine, grapes, figs, and all kinds of burdens, which they brought into Jerusalem on the Sabbath day. And I warned them about the day on which they were selling provisions. Men of Tyre dwelt there also, who brought in fish and all kinds of goods, and sold them on the Sabbath to the children of Judah, and in Jerusalem. Then I contended with the nobles of Judah, and said to them, What evil thing is this that you do, by which you profane the Sabbath day?"* Nehemiah 13:15-17.

Every housewife knows that shopping is extremely wearisome. No one feels rested or refreshed after such activity. This is why the Bible says that shopping (**BUYING AND SELLING**) on the Sabbath violates its sanctity and prevents us from enjoying the blessedness of this special day.

AVOID SECULAR PLEASURES

11. What kind of pleasure should be avoided?

> *"If you turn away your foot from the Sabbath, from doing your pleasure on My holy day, and call the Sabbath a delight, the holy day of the Lord honorable, and shall honor Him, not doing your own ways, nor finding your own pleasure, nor speaking your own words, then you shall delight yourself in the Lord; and I will cause you to ride on the high hills of the earth, and feed you with the heritage of Jacob your father. The mouth of the Lord has spoken."* Isaiah 58:13, 14.

OUR OWN PERSONAL PLEASURES, such as sports and amusements, as well as our own ways (secular chores, hobbies, etc.) are not necessarily wrongful pursuits. Only when engaged in on the Sabbath do they interfere with our relationship with Christ.

Our "own words" refer to business, political, or secular conversations.

WORSHIP GOD AT CHURCH

12. **Where did Jesus always go on the Sabbath?**

"So He came to Nazareth, where He had been brought up. And as His custom was, He went into the synagogue on the Sabbath day, and stood up to read." Luke 4:16.

Jesus habitually attended the local **SYNAGOGUE** on Sabbath mornings, which was the Jewish church of that time. One of the highlights of Sabbath-keeping is to join with believers in group worship. This has great potential for the strengthening of the Sabbath experience, as well as the promotion of our overall experience in holy living. Every reasonable effort should be made to avail ourselves of such spiritual pleasure as worshiping God with a Sabbath-keeping congregation.

QUIZ FOR LESSON NO. 11

List the five activities that are compatible with Sabbath observance:

CHURCH ATTENDANCE
BALL GAME
MOW THE LAWN
BIBLE STUDY
WALK IN NATURE
SHOPPING
REST
GO TO A MOVIE
ENJOY SACRED MUSIC

The Devil's Weapon of Choice
Lesson No. 12

A More Intense Devil

1. **What can we expect from the Devil in these last days?**

   "Therefore rejoice, O heavens, and you who dwell in them! Woe to the inhabitants of the earth and the sea! For the devil has come down to you, having great wrath, because he knows that he has a short time." Revelation 12:12.

The Devil was summarily defeated by Christ on the cross of Calvary. Since Christ has left this earth and ascended back to heaven, the Devil cannot engage Christ Himself any longer. Therefore, he turns his attention upon Christ's followers in **GREAT WRATH**.

These words warn us that the shortness of time left to this world will not weaken or discourage the Devil. Instead, his activities will intensify, and we need to be on high alert in these last days.

His Weapon of Choice

Satan has in his arsenal numerous weapons he uses upon us. Among them are temptations; trials and difficulties; corrupting entertainments, etc. But there is one weapon above all others that he employs to detract people from God and render them unfit for eternal life. We need to be aware of this tactic he uses, for it is the tactic that gives him most success.

2. **Whom is the Devil seeking today?**

   "Be sober, be vigilant; because your adversary the Devil walks about like a roaring lion, seeking whom he may devour." I Peter 5:8.

He is on the loose today in this world, searching for people **HE MAY DEVOUR**. The Devil apparently cannot "devour" just anyone he happens to meet. He must seek out, or look for, probable victims, much as a lion does its prey. One thing is self-evident: Satan is not allowed by God to overpower us with sheer physical force, against our will. No human being would be a match for such a mighty angel as Satan. Instead of physical force, he uses a very lethal weapon of his own invention.

3. How did the Devil gain control of this world?

> *"So the great dragon was cast out, that serpent of old, called the Devil and Satan, who deceives the whole world; he was cast to the earth, and his angels were cast out with him." Revelation 12:9.*

The original weapon the Devil utilized upon human beings was **DECEPTION**. In heaven, force was utilized. He "fought" to gain control. He failed miserably, because his strength was no match for that of God Himself. When Satan turns his full attention upon this world, he found great success in using a different tactic.

4. The Devil is the father of what?

> *"You are of your father the devil, and the desires of your father you want to do. He was a murderer from the beginning, and does not stand in the truth, because there is no truth in him. When he speaks a lie, he speaks from his own resources, for he is a liar and the father of it." John 8:44.*

LIES are the weapon of choice for the Devil. This is an exclusive tool of the Devil. Titus 1:2 says that God is incapable of using this tool. Therefore, using lies, the Devil has an advantage over God. Satan can misrepresent, falsify, and deceive. God must, and will always, tell the truth, even when it is to His disadvantage to do so. Actually, this "disadvantage" turns out to be a tremendous advantage for God's, because it means that He can always be trusted.

5. What did Jesus warn would be the greatest danger to believers during the tribulation?

> *"For then there will be great tribulation, such as has not been since the beginning of the world until this time, no, nor ever shall be. And unless those days were shortened, no flesh would be saved; but for the elect's sake those days will be shortened. Then if anyone says to you, Look, here is the Christ! or there! do not believe it. For false christs and false prophets will rise and show great signs and wonders to deceive, if possible, even the elect." Matthew 24:21-24.*

The Bible warns of many dangers to us today. Worldliness and covetousness are a threat to our spiritual welfare. Persecution and hardship may cause us to lose our hold on God. But more dangerous than any of these is the Devil's most powerful tool: **DECEPTION**.

6. What will deceive many people in the last days?

> *"He performs great signs, so that he even makes fire come down from heaven on the earth in the sight of men. And he deceives those who dwell on the earth by those signs which he was granted to do in the sight of the beast, telling those who dwell on the earth to make an image to the beast who was wounded by the sword and lived." Revelation 13:13, 14.*

According to Revelation 16:14 we will not be able to trust our own eyes, because **SIGNS AND MIRACLES** will be performed by demons themselves. Only the Word of God can be full trusted.

7. Who will the Devil use to deceive others?

> *"But evil men and impostors will grow worse and worse, deceiving and being deceived." II Timothy 3:13.*

EVIL MEN AND IMPOSTERS are the front men for the Devil. Satan himself always remains in the background, out of sight. Most are themselves deceived, and do not view themselves as wrong at all. But because they have been tricked into believing error, they become innocent tools of the Devil to deceive others, in spite of their good intentions.

8. What other group of people can the Devil use to deceive us?

> *"For such are false apostles, deceitful workers, transforming themselves into apostles of Christ. And no wonder! For Satan himself transforms himself into an angel of light. Therefore it is no great thing if his ministers also transform themselves into ministers of righteousness, whose end will be according to their works." II Corinthians 11:13-15.*

Even **PEOPLE CLAIMING TO BE WORKERS FOR CHRIST** can be unwittingly used by the Devil to deceive others. This means that we cannot judge as right and true what someone shares with us merely because he is a pastor or minister who seems very sincere and earnest. Only comparing ideas with the Bible can give us a dependable tool to judge truth from error, right from wrong.

9.   What tool did the Devil use to tempt Jesus?

> *"Then the Devil took Him up into the holy city, set Him on the pinnacle of the temple, and said to Him, If You are the Son of God, throw Yourself down. For it is written: He shall give His angels charge over you, and In their hands they shall bear you up, lest you dash your foot against a stone." Matthew 4:5, 6.*

The Devil does not hesitate to use the Bible if he can twist, or distort it, to serve his own purposes. He made a suggestion to Christ with one or two **BIBLE TEXTS** for support. Jesus protected Himself from the Devil's deception by carefully comparing other Scriptures with the ones in question. We must do the same, or Satan will succeed in using the Bible to deceive us.

10. How is it possible to handle the Word of God?

> *"But we have renounced the hidden things of shame, not walking in craftiness nor handling the word of God deceitfully, but by manifestation of the truth commending ourselves to every man's conscience in the sight of God." II Corinthians 4:2.*

The Bible can be used or misused. The Apostle Paul says it is possible to handle it **DECEITFULLY**. There is a dangerous tolerance today that insists that opposing views are just different ways of seeing things, and the Bible can be used to support anything. If two opposing religious teachings or practices claim Bible support at least one of them must be wrong. By comparing all the Bible has to say on the matter will usually clear up the confusion and one can discern truth from error.

11.   What else is a source of deception for us?

> *"The heart is deceitful above all things, and desperately wicked: who can know it?" Jeremiah 17:9.*

OUR HEARTS can do this better than anything else. Therefore, we should never consult our feelings, when deciding what is right or wrong. To give more authority to a personal experience we have over a plain Bible statement makes us dangerously vulnerable to deception.

Victims

12.   Where will victims of deceit end up?
"Blessed are those who do His commandments, that they may have the right to the tree of life, and may enter through the gates into the city. But outside are dogs and sorcerers and sexually immoral and murderers and idolaters, and whosoever loves and practices a lie." Revelation 22:14, 15.

Here are pictured people who love and practice a lie. They apparently do not think it is a lie, but they have been duped into believing it so. They are victims of someone who lied to them. Innocent though they might have been, they are still held responsible and are pictured as being some day **OUTSIDE THE CITY OF GOD**. So what we choose to believe does make an important difference.

The Devil is too smart to waste so much of his energy on deception, if his victims would be saved anyway. If it did not make any difference to our eternal destiny, Jesus would not have given such dire warnings about falling prey to deception.

13.   What is the fate of those who are deceived?

"The coming of the lawless one is according to the working of Satan, with all power, signs, and lying wonders, and with all unrighteous deception among those who perish, because they did not receive the love of the truth, that they might be saved." II Thessalonians 2:9, 10.

There is an old saying that says, "All roads lead to Rome." Some say this is also true of salvation, "All beliefs lead to salvation." But the Bible maintains that there is only one road to eternal life, and all others lead to destruction. Everyone will not end up in the kingdom of heaven, no matter what they believe. If people are not careful with what they accept as truth **THEY WILL PERISH**.

Nothing could be clearer: receive the truth and be saved, or cherish delusion and perish. Solomon admonished us, "Buy the truth, and do not sell it." Proverbs 23:23.

14. What is the real reason God condemns those who accept lies?

"And for this reason God will send them strong delusion, that they should believe the lie, that they all may be condemned who did not believe the truth but had pleasure in unrighteousness." II Thessalonians 2:11, 12.

The actual reason people who believe lies is because **THEY WOULD NOT BELIEVE THE TRUTH.** In the end, God will not condemn us because we were in error, but because we rejected the truth when we heard it, choosing to cling to our old ideas, traditions, or way of life. Rejection of truth always paves the way for us to be deceived into believing lies.

15. What will truth do to us?

"Sanctify them by Your truth. Your word is truth." John 17:17.

Now we can see why the Bible is so concerned with falsehood and warns us so strongly about it. Truth does something for us falsehood can never do. It is able to **SANCTIFY US**. When we understand and obey the truth of God, it brings a holy, uplifting influence into our lives. It animates our soul with a captivating spiritual power, and renders the Devil powerless to attract us. In John 8:32 Jesus says, "And you shall know the truth, and the truth shall make you free."

QUIZ FOR LESSON NO. 12

Unscramble:

1. CEPDETNIO: This is the devil's weapon of choice.

2. BBELI: This is a tool the devil does not hesitate to use.

3. RUTTH: We cannot be saved if we reject it.

4. ISHPER: What will be the fate of all who cherish ideas they know are untrue?

5. RTHEA: This is untrustworthy in deciding what is right or wrong.

The Pale Horse   [THE FOURTH SEAL]
Lesson No. 13

We have concluded our study of the tribulation which contained a death threat to all who continue obeying God's Ten Commandments. This will test everyone's faith in God, and was represented in the third seal by the black horse rider carrying a pair of scales, "to test those who dwell on the earth."

Now we will turn our attention to the next seal and its elaboration farther on in the book of Revelation.

The Fourth Horse

1.   What was the color of the fourth horse?

   "When He opened the fourth seal, I heard the voice of the fourth living creature saying, Come and see. So I looked, and behold, a pale horse. And the name of him who sat on it was Death, and Hades followed with him." Revelation 6:7, 8.

This horse is of an unusual color, the text says it was **PALE**. Modern versions of the Bible use very vivid words to attempt to convey the true nature of this Greek word for "pale," such as "pale green like a corpse," "sickly green," or "ashen." It is clear that this pale horse is not a pleasant pastel shade, but the ghastly pallor of disease and death.

Since the color of each of the four horses is a key to the experience it represents, we are naturally inquisitive about the color of this fourth horse. It is not a normal color, but one of disease and death.

2.   What four weapons will these riders use?

   "And power was given to them over a fourth of the earth, to kill with sword, with hunger, with death, and by the beasts of the earth." Revelation 6:8.

The riders on this horse wield more weaponry than any of the other horse riders. Their arsenal includes **[1] SWORD, [2] HUNGER** (famine), **[3] DEATH** (disease), and **[4] BEASTS**.

These weapons are portrayed elsewhere in Scripture as God's four special tools of judgment upon disobedient people in the past. The word "death," mentioned two times, is the Greek word "thanatos," which means pestilence or disease.

Let us go back in Scripture and read how God used these very same weapons upon unfaithful people.

3. **What four weapons did Moses say God would use to punish the Israelites, if they became disobedient after they entered Canaan?**

"I will also send wild beasts among you, which shall rob you of your children, destroy your livestock, and make you few in number; and your highways shall be desolate. And if by these things you are not reformed by Me, but walk contrary to Me, then I also will walk contrary to you, and I will punish you yet seven times for your sins. And I will bring a sword against you that will execute the vengeance of the covenant; when you are gathered together within your cities I will send pestilence among you; and you shall be delivered into the hand of the enemy. When I have cut off your supply of bread, ten women shall bake weight, and you shall eat and not be satisfied." Leviticus 26:22-26.

Here are the very same weapons, but used in a slightly different order. [1] **WILD BEASTS**; [2] **SWORD**; [3] **PESTILENCE**; and [4] **HUNGER** (famine).

Notice the source of these punishments. While it is an accepted fact that the Devil often uses these very weapons to bring misery, suffering, and death upon the human race, it is also a clear scriptural teaching that God Himself at times uses these deadly instruments to punish gross disobedience.

4. **In Ezekiel's time, what four judgments would God use to punish a disobedient Jerusalem?**

"For thus says the Lord God: How much more it shall be when I send My four severe judgments on Jerusalem---the sword and famine and wild beasts and pestilence---to cut off man and beast from it?" Ezekiel 14:21.

Once again is pictured these four weapons, in yet a different sequence. [1] **SWORD**; [2] **FAMINE** (hunger); [3] **WILD BEASTS**; and [4] **PES-**

TILENCE. So when we meet these special instruments of judgment in Revelation, they are not strangers to us, because Revelation pictures God using them once again in the closing days of earth's history.

We are now studying the fourth seal, the pale horse with its twin riders wielding four deadly weapons. In our study of Revelation thus far, we have learned that these seven seals are, in symbolic form, but short, cryptic descriptions of seven major events during the time of the end. We have also discovered that the subsequent chapters of Revelation reveal a more expanded, detailed account of those events --- in the same order. This would mean that Chapters 15 and 16, which describe the seven last plagues, should give us additional light about the work of these pale horse riders.

Seal	Explanation
1 – White Horse	Chapter 7
2 – Red Horse	Chapters 8-11
3 – Black Horse	Chapters 12-14
4 – Pale Horse	Chapter 15 , 16

5. Whose wrath is shown in the seven last plagues?

   "Then I saw another sign in heaven, great and marvelous: seven angels having the seven last plagues, for in them the wrath of God is complete." Revelation 15:1.

It is right and proper for Christians to highlight God's *love* for man. Souls are loved, not scared, into the kingdom of God. However, Revelation pictures another side of God's character that must not be ignored: His *justice*. These plagues are a punishment so severe that many find it difficult to believe that God is involved at all. However, they are plainly called the wrath of **GOD**, not the wrath of the Devil, or man.

6. As He proceeds with this punishment, how is God described by onlookers who are not involved?

   "And I heard the angel of the waters saying: You are righteous, O Lord, the One who is and who was and who is to be, because You have judged these things. For they have shed the blood of saints and prophets, and You have given them blood to drink. For it is their just due. And I heard another from the altar saying, Even so, Lord God Almighty, true and righteous are Your judgments." Revelation 16:5-7.

It is clear that these onlookers are not upset with God for what He is doing. On the contrary, they declare Him **RIGHTEOUS**, justified in pouring out these judgments upon His earthly enemies in the last days.

These judgments are not the result of God losing control of His temper and doing some very irrational things to human beings. Those who witness these outpourings of divine judgments are very supportive of God's actions at this time.

When?

It is important that we ascertain the time frame for these plague judgments to fall. As we carefully study the narrative we can find two clues as to when these plagues will be poured out. The first clue is found in the introductory vision to these seven last plagues.

7. **While the plagues are falling, who will be able to enter heaven's temple to intercede for mercy?**

    "The temple was filled with smoke from the glory of God and from His power, and no one was able to enter the temple till the seven plagues of the seven angels were completed." Revelation 15:8

Sometimes the Old Testament priests could not enter the earthly temple to do their daily intercessory act of offering incense because of a great manifestation of glory from God. Similarly, the same type of imagery is used in Revelation to picture the cessation of heavenly intercession for mankind by Jesus, our Great High Priest. **NO ONE** was able to enter the true, heavenly temple while these plagues were doing their work on earth.

Christ ceases His work of intercession in the heavenly temple just prior to these plagues. The door of human probation will be closed for good, and all opportunity to repent will be gone. This is why it is stated twice that no repentance occurs as a result of these punishments. See Revelation 16:9, 11.

8. **Who are the first victims of these plagues?**

    "So the first went and poured out his bowl upon the earth, and a foul and loathsome sore came upon the men who had the mark of the beast and those who worshiped his image." Revelation 16:2.

Here is the second clue that helps us see just when these plagues are poured out. **THOSE WHO HAD THE MARK OF THE BEAST** were the first ones to be targeted. This means that by this time everyone has made his final decision and received either the seal of God, or the beast's mark. This results in the close of human probation, a short time before Christ arrives back to this earth in power and great glory.

"Revelation 13:3 declares that "All the world marveled and followed the beast." The beast will convince the masses of its agenda. In order for the beast to deceive people, it must put on a very charming, Christian face and pose as a great champion for God. Now, however, the whole world will discern between the "one who serves God and the one who does not serve Him." Malachi 3:18.

We will now survey these plagues, which are seven in number.

PLAGUE NO. 1
9. **What breaks out on those who have the mark?**

   "So the first went and poured out his bowl upon the earth and a foul and loathsome sore came upon the men who had the mark of the beast and those who worshiped his image." Revelation 16:2.

A FOUL AND LOATHSOME SORE breaks out only on those who accept the mark of the beast and his image. Commandment keepers will be exonerated immediately, since they are all exempt from this painful disease. It will then be made clear that God honors them, not the beast and his image.

These people thought the easy way was to obey the Antichrist beast, assuming that God would understand. Too late they will discover that their choice was actually the hard way.

PLAGUE NO. 2
10. **What will happen to water in the sea?**

    "Then the second angel poured out his bowl on the sea, and it became as of a dead man, and every living creature in the sea died." Revelation 16:3.

Now the focus of attention is on the sea water. **IT BECOMES BLOOD**, no doubt resulting in stench and disease. The distress from this situation will be felt most keenly by beach resorts and seaports, which are today some of the greatest hotbeds of sin.

PLAGUE NO. 3
11. What else will turn bloody?

> *"Then the third angel poured out his bowl on the rivers and springs of water, and they became blood." Revelation 16:4.*

RIVERS AND SPRINGS are now contaminated. Those living inland from the seashores will now be impacted by the same foul stench.

PLAGUE NO. 4
12. What causes more suffering?

> *"Then the fourth angel poured out his bowl on the sun, and power was given to him to scorch men with fire. And men were scorched with great heat, and they blasphemed the name of God who has power over these plagues; and they did not repent and give Him glory." Revelation 16:8, 9.*

THE SCORCHING OF THE SUN becomes a problem. No doubt God removes the ozone layer, or some other adjustment in the atmosphere, to allow the full strength of the sun's rays to reach earth. The sun's scorching, fiery blast will wither plant life, sicken animals, and bring on famine.

PLAGUE NO. 5
13. What specific place is targeted by this plague?

> *"Then the fifth angel poured out his bowl on the throne of the beast, and his kingdom became full of darkness; and they gnawed their tongues because of the pain. They blasphemed the God of heaven because of their pains and their sores, and did not repent of their deeds." Revelation 16:10, 11.*

We learned that **THE THRONE OF THE BEAST** was given him by the Roman dragon long years ago. The beast's throne is doubtless its headquarters, with all its high-ranking leaders reverenced by all the world. Thus exposed, these once pious leaders turn against God Himself.

PLAGUE NO. 6
14. Whom do the three trouble-makers convince to come together into one united coalition?

> *"Then the sixth angel poured out his bowl on the great river Euphrates, and its water was dried up, so that the way of the kings from the east might be prepared. And I saw three unclean spirits like frogs coming out of the mouth of the dragon, out of the mouth of the beast, and out of the mouth of the false prophet. For they are spirits of demons, performing signs, which go out to the kings of the earth and of the whole world, to gather them to the battle of that great day of God Almighty. Behold, I am coming as a thief. Blessed is he who watches, and keeps his garments, lest he walk naked and they see his shame. And they gathered them together to the place called in Hebrew, Armageddon."* Revelation 16:12-16.

For the one and only time **THE KINGS OF THE WHOLE WORLD** cease fighting each other and begin to work together for a common goal. These political powers cease their in-fighting and come together in a massive military build-up for confrontation with a common enemy --- God. The battle they will fight will be their last. It is described later in Revelation 17:14 and 19:19.

PLAGUE NO. 7
15.   What announcement is proclaimed at the last plague?

> *"Then the seventh angel poured out his bowl into the air, and a loud voice came out of the temple of heaven, from the throne, saying, It is done! And there were noises and thunderings and lightnings; and there was a great earthquake, such a mighty and great earthquake as had not occurred since men were on the earth. Now the great city was divided into three parts, and the cities of the nations fell. And great Babylon was remembered before God, to give her the cup of the wine of the fierceness of His wrath. Then every island fled away and the mountains were not found. And great hail from heaven fell upon men, each hailstone about the weight of a talent. Men blasphemed God because of the plague of the hail, since that plague was exceedingly great."* Revelation 16:17-21.

On the cross He cried out the words, "It is finished!" as He concluded His work on earth for man's salvation. Now that He has concluded His work in heaven for man's salvation, a similar cry of conclusion rings out, "**IT IS DONE**!"

QUIZ FOR LESSON NO. 13

Choose the Right Answer:

1. Seven last plagues are the wrath of:
    (A) Man
    (B) The Devil
    (C) God

2. When will these plagues fall on mankind?
    (A) After probation closes for man
    (B) Before probation closes for man
    (C) After the coming of Christ

3. Victims of the first plague:
    (A) Those who have God's seal
    (B) Those who have the beast's mark
    (C) Satan and his fallen angels

4. Why will God pour out these plagues?
    (A) He loses control of Himself and overreacts
    (B) Good angels push Him to do it
    (C) It's because of mankind's wicked behavior

5. Color of the fourth horse that represents these plagues:
    (A) Red
    (B) Black
    (C) Pale Green

Praying Martyrs
Lesson No. 14

The Fifth Seal

1. **Who appear when the fifth seal is opened?**

   "When He opened the fifth seal, I saw under the altar the souls of those who had been slain for the word of God and for the testimony which they held. And they cried with a loud voice, saying, How long, O Lord, holy and true, until You judge and avenge our blood on those who dwell on the earth? Then a white robe was given to each of them; and it was said to them that they should rest a little while longer, until both the number of their fellow servants and their brethren, who would be killed as they were, was completed." Revelation 6:9-11.

   Not horses, but **PRAYING MARTYRS** are the focus of attention in this seal. A martyr is a person who is murdered because of his religious beliefs, not someone who dies while trying to kill others because of their religious beliefs.

2. **Who were these martyrs? When did they lose their lives because of their religious convictions? We have several groups we could choose from.**

   [1] There were the martyrs of Old Testament times. Jesus referred to them when He said to the Jews of His day, "Woe to you, scribes and Pharisees, hypocrites! Because you build the tombs of the prophets and adorn the monuments of the righteous, and say, If we had lived in the days of our fathers, we would not have been partakers with them in the blood of the prophets. Therefore you are witnesses against yourselves that you are sons of those who murdered the prophets." Matthew 23:29-31

   [2] Then there were many of the early Christians who lost their lives in the first centuries of the Christian church, when the pagan Roman Empire raged an all-out war against them, often feeding devout Christians to the hungry lions in their sports arenas for entertainment.

[3] Also there were the millions who suffered martyrdom during the long papal persecutions for 1260 years. By some estimates more than 50 million endured this difficult time, often burned alive at the stake.

[4] But these martyrs pictured in Revelation are a separate group. If we pay close attention to what the passage is saying, we will quickly see that these are future martyrs, those who will be called upon to give up their lives rather than give up their faith.

Notice carefully that there is not one, but three distinct groups of people mentioned in this seal.

The Three Groups

THE FIRST GROUP: Already slain:

*". . . those who **HAD BEEN** slain." Verse 9.*

It is crucial to observe the language used to describe these dead Christians. It indicates that they were not slain *after*, or even *during*, but *before* the seal was opened. It pictures their slaying as an already accomplished event.

THE SECOND GROUP: About to be killed:

*". . . who **WOULD BE killed** as they were." Verse 11.*

This group is still alive, but facing eminent death. Other Bible versions make this clear by translating the Greek tense of this verb more precisely:
"were to be killed" – NIV
"about to be killed" - Interlinear Bible
"should be killed" – KJV

THE THIRD GROUP: The Killers:

3. How do the martyrs describe their murderers?

    "And they cried with a loud voice, saying, How long, O Lord, holy and true, until You judge and avenge our blood on those who dwell on the earth?" Revelation 6:10.

They are referred to as **THOSE WHO DWELL ON THE EARTH**. The Greek word indicates present, on-going action and should be translated "those dwelling on the earth. The sense of the Greek is that those responsible for the death of these martyrs are not pictured as being dead themselves, but alive and "dwelling on the earth" --- an expression used for people alive at this time. Therefore, they cannot be the dead persecutors of long-ago Medieval times.

Taking into consideration all these details, we can come to a safe conclusion that all three of these groups are end-time groups. Let us look more closely at each of these groups, taking into consideration what the rest of the book of Revelation reveals about these end-time martyrs and their murderers.

The First Group

4. Why does God turn some peoples' drinking water into blood during the third plague?

   "And I heard the angel of the waters saying: You are righteous, O Lord, the One who is and who was and who is to be, because You have judged these things. For they have shed the blood of saints and prophets, and You have given them blood to drink. For it is their just due." Revelation 16:5, 6.

This prophecy indicates that deadly force will be used once again in these last days of earth's history. The reason given for some to endure these terrible plagues is because **THEY HAVE SHED THE BLOOD OF SAINTS AND PROPHETS**. No wonder Jesus warned us, saying, "For then there will be great tribulation, such as has not been since the beginning of the world until this time, no, nor ever shall be" Matthew 24:21.

None of the papal leaders of Medieval times will experience any of the seven last plagues, because they will all still be in their graves at the time when these plagues are poured out on the last generation of persecutors. The only conclusion we can come to is that these murderers are end-time sinners and the people they murdered must be end-time people as well.

5. What will be the fate of some who refuse to receive the mark of the beast?

> *"And I saw thrones, and they sat on them, and judgment was committed to them. Then I saw the souls of those who had been beheaded for their witness to Jesus and for the word of God, who had not worshiped the beast or his image, and had not received his mark on their foreheads or on their hands. And they lived and reigned with Christ for a thousand years."* Revelation 20:4.

The mark of the beast and his image are end-time, not ancient or Medieval problems for God's commandment keeping people. This text says that some will be **BEHEADED** for their resistance to that beast. Once again we see evidence that when this beast emerges into worldwide fame and authority, there will be martyrdom experienced by some in these last days,

Some look upon religious persecution as a relic of the Dark Ages. They reason that people never need worry about having to die for one's faith in this modern time of enlightenment, freedom, and tolerance. However, the book of Revelation reveals otherwise.

The Second Group

6. What is the second group called?

> *"Then a white robe was given to each of them; and it was said to them that they should rest a little while longer, until both the number of their fellow servants and their brethren, who would be killed as they were, was completed."* Revelation 6:11.

These, who were once companions of the dead martyrs, are described as **FELLOW SERVANTS and BRETHREN**. The biblical term "fellow servant" is always used to describe people who were contemporaries, serving alongside each other. See Colossians 4:7. It is not used to refer to one's spiritual forefathers. This makes both the dead martyrs and living fellow servants, end-time believers.

7. What impending fate do these living saints face?

> *"He was granted power to give breath to the image of the beast, that the image of the beast should both speak and cause as many as would not worship the image of the beast to be killed."* Revelation 13:15.

The "image of the beast" will "cause" (enact a law) making provision for all violators **TO BE KILLED**. A death decree will finally be enacted, with a near-future execution date, but God will not allow all His faithful people to be martyred. We know this is so from another Scripture in Revelation.

8. **Who will be protected during the fifth trumpet?**
"They were commanded not to harm the grass of the earth, or any green thing, or any tree, but only those men who do not have the seal of God on their foreheads." Revelation 9:4.

THOSE WHO HAVE THE SEAL OF GOD on their foreheads are under divine protection. Since the trumpet events all occur after the close of human probation, at least some of God's people will be spared martyrdom. The martyrs of the fifth seal apparently lost their lives during the first seal, before probation closed. At that time a great spiritual revival will swell to a loud cry, and those responding to God's call will receive God's seal of approval. It is during this spiritual struggle with the beast when its mark of authority is exposed as false, that the fifth seal martyrs die.

The Third Group

How God would answer the prayer of the martyrs for justice is not given in the fifth seal, but later in the book, in the explanatory section for that seal.

Seal	Explanation
1 – White Horse	Chapter 7
2 – Red Horse	Chapters 8-11
3 – Black Horse	Chapters 12-14
4 – Pale Horse	Chapters 15, 16
5 – Praying Martyrs	Chapters 1, 18

As we look into those explanatory chapters of the fifth seal (chapters 17 and 18) we will easily be able to identify this third group---the murderers of those martyrs. We shall also see how God will answer those martyrs' prayers.

9. **Who is being judged in this vision?**

"Then one of the seven angels who had the seven bowls came and talked with me, saying to me, Come, I will show you the judgment of the great harlot who sits on many waters." Revelation 17:1.

When this section begins, John is introduced to **THE GREAT HARLOT**. She is the center of attention for chapters 17 and 18. She is revealed as the one responsible for the death of many who were faithful to God, and for this reason she will be punished and destroyed.

Chapters 17 and 18 picture the judgment of an entity symbolized by an immoral woman. She does not represent those who are sexually unfaithful to their husbands, but she is a symbol of all those who are spiritually unfaithful to Christ and His Word. Since a woman is used in Scripture to represent God's church (O.T.: "daughter of Zion" and N.T.: "bride of Christ") this woman pictures a church that has been unfaithful to God by ignoring His Ten Commandments, thus a "harlot."

10. **What caused this woman to be drunk?**

> *"I saw the woman, drunk with the blood of the saints and with the blood of the martyrs of Jesus. And when I saw her, I marveled with great amazement." Revelation 17:6.*

This "harlot," who is drunk with "**THE BLOOD OF SAINTS**," is the same entity as the beast of Revelation 13 who makes "war with the saints" and overcomes them. She is also identical with the "little horn" of Daniel 7, which "was making war against the saints and prevailing against them."

11. **Who does God use to bring the entity represented by this woman to her end?**

> *"And the ten horns which you saw on the beast, these will hate the harlot, make her desolate and naked, eat her flesh and burn her with fire. For God has put it into their hearts to fulfill His purpose, to be of one mind, and to give their kingdom to the beast, until the words of God are fulfilled." Revelation 17:16, 17.*

These **TEN HORNS** represent the western European nations which emerged out of the Roman Empire, represented by a ten-horned dragon in both Daniel and Revelation. These political nations, once heavily influenced by her, will turn on her and bring her to a violent end. It was one of those horns (France) that inflicted the deadly wound on the Papacy in 1798, almost annihilating it. In the interim, the mortal wound healed and did not kill it, but in the end all the horn powers will unite in making sure there is no future for this persecuting power.

12. **What other punishment will she receive?**

   "Therefore her plagues will come in one day---death and mourning and famine. And she will be utterly burned with fire, for strong is the Lord God who judges her." Revelation 18:8.

She is getting trouble from two sources: man and God. God deals out to her **PLAGUES**, and stands back and does not interfere when her former admirers burn her with fire.

13. **Who orchestrated this vengeance upon her?**

   "Rejoice over her, O heaven, and you holy apostles and prophets, for God has avenged you on her! Then a mighty angel took up a stone like a great millstone and threw it into the sea, saying, Thus with violence the great city Babylon shall be thrown down, and shall not be found anymore." Revelation 18:20, 21.

Thus will **GOD** answer the prayer of those martyrs for vengeance on their murderers. "Vengeance is Mine, I will repay says the Lord." Romans 12:19

QUIZ FOR LESSON NO. 14

Choose the right group:

    (A) Those already killed
    (B) Those about to be killed
    (C) Those who do the killing

1. Who were the first people group John saw when the fifth seal was opened?

2. Who were the fellow servants of the slain martyrs?

3. God will use the nations of the world to punish what group?

4. What people group was mentioned in explanatory chapters 17 and 18?

5. Who were the people represented by the great harlot?

Do Dead People Pray?
Lesson No. 15

We learned in our last lesson that when the fifth seal was opened, John was shown some dead martyrs conversing with God about their plight. This raises a logical question: Do dead people and God converse together? Are dead people imprisoned under an altar in heaven, rather than having freedom to move about?

It is extremely helpful to check with other Scriptures to arrive at a proper answer. Before arriving at an interpretation of some item in a prophecy, we must always first ask the question, "Is this literal or symbolic?" The rule is that it is literal, unless proven otherwise. If it is irrational or impossible to consider it literal, then it must be symbolic. With this principle in mind, let us revisit this fifth seal and compare other Scriptures with our conclusion.

Literal or Symbolic?

1. **Where are martyrs pictured as being?**

   "When He opened the fifth seal, I saw under the altar the souls of those who had been slain for the word of God and for the testimony which they held." Revelation 6:9.

These souls are pictured as residing **UNDER THE ALTAR**. We are not told precisely just where this altar is, but most students of prophecy place this altar in heaven, for these people are dead and, according to their belief, dead people who are good, end up there.

It is apparent that John was shown pictorial representations. When people go to heaven they are not imprisoned under some altar. Therefore, it would not make sense to view them as literal, disembodied spirits, alive and praying in heaven.

2. **What were these martyrs told to do "a little while longer?"**

> *"Then a white robe was given to each of them; and it was said to them that they should rest a little while longer, until both the number of their fellow servants and their brethren, who would be killed as they were, was completed." Revelation 6:11.*

They are told to **REST** a while longer. They are not pictured as being active, or moving about in normal activity. It is easy to conclude that their resting is literal, for many other Bible statements support this concept.

3. What will those who die in the Lord do at death?

> *"Then I heard a voice from heaven saying to me, Write: Blessed are the dead who die in the Lord from now on. Yes, says the Sprit, that they may rest from their labors, and their works follow them." Revelation 14:13.*

Revelation is consistent with all descriptions in Scripture regarding what a person is doing while dead. It is apparent that the language used here is literal when it says that they **REST FROM THEIR LABORS.**

The correct Bible teaching is that death is a state of restful and undisturbed quietness, like going to sleep, until awakening at the resurrection.

4. What cried out to God after Abel was killed?

> *"And He said, What have you done? The voice of your brother's blood cries out to Me from the ground." Genesis 4:10.*

God said that **ABEL'S BLOOD** was crying out to Him from the ground. We must understand this crying out to be symbolic, and not literal, since literal blood does not have intelligence, or a voice. It would be irrational to understand this Scripture otherwise.

Death in the Bible

The book of Revelation fully agrees with the rest of the Bible which pictures death as a restful sleep, rather than an immediate entrance into another, highly active life. What we are about to learn in the last part of the book of Revelation will be confusing to us unless we clear up our thinking about this matter.

Amazingly, Christians today are taught the very opposite. They are taught that the moment a believer dies he enters promptly into a new, higher and very active life. Since this teaching is so popular today, it would be good for us to survey the Bible's teaching about this.

5. **What do dead people NOT do?**

> *"The dead do not praise the Lord, nor any who go down into silence." Psalm 115:17.*

It is inconceivable that if dead believers do enter heaven at their death, they would totally ignore God and would not **PRAISE THE LORD**. On the contrary, this Scripture makes a point of their ending up in silence, rather than joining the angels in their songs of praise to God.

6. **What do dead people know?**

> *"For the living know that they will die; but the dead know nothing, and they have no more reward, for the memory of them is forgotten. Also their love, their hatred, and their envy have now perished; nevermore will they have a share in anything done under the sun." Ecclesiastes 9:5, 6.*

People know a lot of things while alive in this world, but once they slip under the power of death, they know **NOTHING**. The reason for this lack on their part is that they are asleep. "Sleep" is the favorite Bible expression to describe a dead person. More than 50 times it is so used in Scripture. Death is not passing into another life in a more delightful (or frightful) world of existence.

7. **When Jesus returns what are dead believers doing?**

> *"But I do not want you to be ignorant, brethren, concerning those who have fallen asleep, lest you sorrow as others who have no hope. For if we believe that Jesus died and rose again, even so God will bring with Him those who sleep in Jesus. For this we say to you by the word of the Lord, that we who are alive and remain until the coming of the Lord will by no means precede those who are asleep." I Thessalonians 4:13-15.*

The Apostle Paul believed that when people died they were **SLEEPING**. Death is man's enemy, because it prevents us from communicating with God or one another. Yet, it has some beautiful advantages. As in our nightly sleep, it will seem to us that one moment we fall asleep in death, and the next moment we awake in the resurrection to participate in the rapture. While dead, we are totally unaware of any sorrow, hardship, or grief our death has brought upon our loved ones, nor will we be troubled by the subsequent struggles of those still living.

The Awakening

8.   When will all believers go to be with Christ?

"Let not your heart be troubled; you believe in God, believe also in Me. In My Father's house are many mansions; if it were not so, I would have told you. I go to prepare a place for you. And if I go and prepare a place for you, I will come again and receive you to Myself; that where I am, there you may be also." John 14:1-3.

At our death, we don't go to heaven one by one, but we go to heaven together **WHEN JESUS COMES AGAIN**. If believers go to heaven one by one at their death, Christ's promise to someday come and get them is meaningless.

9.   What will happen to resurrected believers and living believers at Christ's appearing?

"For this we say to you by the Lord, that we who are alive and remain until the coming of the Lord will by no means precede those who are asleep. For the Lord Himself will descend from heaven with a shout, with the voice of an archangel, and with the trumpet of God. And the dead in Christ will rise first. Then we who are alive and remain shall be caught up together with them in the clouds to meet the Lord in the air. And thus we shall always be with the Lord." I Thessalonians 4:15-17.

It is clear that if we die, a resurrection is necessary before we can go to heaven. The Bible picture is that when the dead believers go to heaven, living saints will be **CAUGHT UP TOGETHER** with them.

It is at the rapture, not at our death, that we will go to our reward and be with the Lord forever. We do not go one by one at the point of death, but all together at the glorious return of Christ.

10. **What will we do as soon as we awake on the resurrection morning?**

> *"Your dead shall live; together with my dead body they shall arise. Awake and sing, you who dwell in dust; for your dew is like the dew of herbs, and the earth shall cast out the dead." Isaiah 26:19.*

What a rapturous joy will surge through our minds the very moment we awaken from the dead and realize that we are alive once again, this time forever! When we came into this life the first time at birth, all the joy and exuberance of that exciting moment was experienced by family and friends. But on the resurrection day we will awaken and break out into **SINGING.** We'll always remember and cherish those first glorious moments of eternity for us.

Some Exceptions

It is also clear from the Bible that there are a few living believers already in heaven, enjoying their eternal reward. However, they are exceptions, not the rule, and they are all specifically mentioned in Scripture.

11. **Who was the first person to enter heaven without dying?**

> *"So all the days of Enoch were three hundred and sixty-five years. And Enoch walked with God; and he was not, for God took him." Genesis 5:23, 24.*

Since there was no death involved for **ENOCH**, it is safe to say that he could not be one of those praying martyrs of the fifth seal. He was one of only two people to by-pass death and enter directly into heaven.

12. What was the subject of a dispute?

> *"Yet Michael the archangel, in contending with the devil, when he disputed about the body of Moses, dared not bring against him a reviling accusation, but said, The Lord rebuke you!"* Jude 9.

This argument over **MOSES' BODY** indicated a special resurrection so that he could be taken to heaven. We know this, because Moses returned to earth hundreds of years later to talk personally with Christ. See Matthew 17:1-3.

13. Who interrupted death's reign?

> *"Nevertheless death reigned from Adam to Moses, even over those who had not sinned according to the likeness of the transgression of Adam, who is a type of Him who was to come."* Romans 5:14.

MOSES was the first to reach heaven after death, but notice that his body was involved.

14. Who else was taken to heaven without dying?

> *"And so it was, when they had crossed over, that Elijah said to Elisha, Ask! What may I do for you, before I am taken away from you? Elisha said, Please let a double portion of your spirit be upon me. So he said, You have asked a hard thing. Nevertheless, if you see me when I am taken from you, it shall be so for you; but if not, it shall not be so. Then it happened, as they continued on and talked, that suddenly a chariot of fire appeared with horses of fire, and separated the two of them; and Elijah went up by a whirlwind into heaven."* II Kings 2:9-11.

We have learned thus far of three individuals in heaven----Enoch, Moses, and **ELIJAH**. However, Revelation pictures a greater number than that.

15. How many more people did John see in heaven?

> *"Immediately I was in the Spirit; and behold, a throne set in heaven, and One sat on the throne. And He who sat there was like a*

> *jasper and a sardius stone in appearance; and there was a rainbow around the throne, in appearance like an emerald. Around the throne were twenty-four elders sitting, clothed in white robes; and they had crowns of gold on their heads." Revelation 4:2-4.*

Here is a sizeable group, **TWENTY-FOUR** in number, whom John sees in heaven already, ahead of the rapture of the future. It is clear that these are living human beings, for they sing about their salvation in Revelation 4:9. We have a good idea who these people are when we examine Scripture.

16. Who were resurrected at Jesus' resurrection?

> *"And Jesus cried out again with a loud voice, and yielded up His spirit. Then, behold, the veil of the temple was torn in two from top to bottom; and the earth quaked and the rocks were split, and the graves were opened; and many bodies of the saints who had fallen asleep were raised; and coming out of the graves after His resurrection, they went into the holy city and appeared to many." Matthew 27:50-53.*

MANY SLEEPING SAINTS were resurrected with bodies. They did not come "down" from heaven. They came "up" out of their graves.

17. When Jesus ascended to heaven who did He take with Him?

> *"Therefore He says: When He ascended on high, He led captivity captive, and gave gifts to men." Ephesians 4:8.*

Jesus did not ascend to heaven alone. He took with him some individuals who were recently **CAPTIVES** of the grave, but now are under His personal control. These special people were hand-selected by Christ Himself, and John sees them enthroned around God in heaven.

These were "first fruits," a small sample of a future harvest of souls in the great rapture of believers when Christ comes again to take us also to the same place --- "where He is." Thus we see that all those whom the Bible pictured as already in their heavenly reward can be accounted for as exceptions, clearly mentioned in Scripture. But the greater number of the redeemed among men await in their graves the coming of Jesus to take them also to heaven, where they will join those who have gone on before.

QUIZ FOR LESSON NO. 15

True or False:

1. The fifth seal features praying martyrs, rather than horses.

2. We know that the martyrs are symbolic, rather than literal people praying in heaven, because the Bible says that the dead know nothing.

3. Believers who are dead do not go to heaven at their death, but when Jesus comes again to resurrect and rapture them.

4. There are no human beings alive in heaven right now.

5. When a believer dies he goes immediately to his heavenly reward.

The Invasion of Planet Earth
Lesson No. 16

The Sixth Seal

When the sixth seal is opened it becomes immediately apparent that the earth is under violent attack. None of the upheavals portrayed could be the responsibility of human beings. They are all supernatural events.

1. **What six phenomena take place?**

    "I looked when He opened the sixth seal, and behold, there was a great earthquake; and the sun became black as sackcloth of hair, and the moon became like blood. And the stars of heaven fell to the earth, as a fig tree drops its late figs when it is shaken by a mighty wind. Then the sky receded as a scroll when it is rolled up, and every mountain and island was moved out of its place." Revelation 6:12-14.

All of this violence happening in rapid succession presents a picture of total chaos and confusion. They are remarkable phenomena and global in extent. [1] **A GREAT EARTHQUAKE**; [2] **SUN BECAME BLACK**; [3] **MOON BECAME LIKE BLOOD**; [4] **STARS FELL**; [5] **SKY RECEDED AS A SCROLL**; and [6] **MOUNTAINS AND ISLANDS MOVED**.

These catastrophic events are not original with Revelation. There are ten texts in the Bible that mention these events. In each of these texts some events are omitted. No text has them all, except the one here in Revelation. They are: Isaiah 13:10-13; Ezekiel 32:7, 8; Joel 2:10; Joel 2:28-31; Joel 3:15, 16; Matthew 24:29; Mark 13:24, 25; Luke 21:25; Acts 2:17-20; and Revelation 6:12-14.

2. **When did Jesus say these signs would appear?**

    "But in those days, after that tribulation, the sun will be darkened, and the moon will not give its light; the stars of heaven will fall, and the powers in the heavens will be shaken." Mark 13:24, 25.

These supernatural signs are tied to the end of a period of tribulation. Jesus said we could look for them to occur **IN THOSE DAYS, AFTER THAT TRIBULATION**.

There are two periods of tribulation mentioned in the prophecies: one is a very long period of 1260 years, ending in 1798, and a very short, intense period of unknown length, just before the return of Christ. About 18 years before the end of that 1260-year period of distress, on May 19, 1780, what many historians call the "Dark Day," occurred. The following night the moon appeared blood-red. Fifty-three years after that, on November 13, 1833, a great meteoric shower took place, more extensive and spectacular than was ever before recorded. These supernatural events exactly matched the Savior's predictions, both as to time and events. At that time a great interest was aroused in the prophecies predicting the second coming of Christ, and a deep spiritual revival occurred, known in history as the Great Second Advent Awakening. Out of that emerged a powerful segment of believers who became known as "Adventists."

In the gospels Jesus associated these signs with the termination of the long 1260-year tribulation. Also in Revelation, Jesus associated these signs with the tribulation time immediately before His second coming. By looking carefully at Jesus' words in the Gospel about these signs to occur, together with their mention in the original Old Testament passages, we can see that these phenomena will be repeated. Let us now look at this biblical evidence which indicates another yet future occurrence of these phenomena, as Revelation predicts.

A Second Occurrence

3. What did Jesus say about the generation who would witness these end-time events?

    "Assuredly, I say to you, this generation will by no means pass away till all these things take place." Mark 13:30.

This is an interesting statement by Jesus, and a very significant one. He says that the generation who witnesses these events **WILL SEE ALL, NOT JUST SOME OF THEM.**

All who witnessed these early signs have passed away. This portion of Jesus' prophecy was not fulfilled. This is evidence that we are to expect these supernatural events to be repeated with the new generation, who will actually witness "the Son of Man coming in the clouds with great power and glory (verse 26)." Indeed, the sixth seal pictures these events as reoccurring, this time in rapid succession, climaxing in the arrival of Christ. A study of some of the Old Testament texts mentioning these phenomena support Revelation's picture.

A Future Dark Day

4. What two events precede the darkening of the sun?

> *"And it shall come to pass afterward that I will pour out My spirit on all flesh; your sons and your daughters shall prophesy, your old men shall dream dreams, your young men shall see visions, and also on My menservants and on My maidservants I will pour out My Spirit in those days. And I will show wonders in the heavens and in the earth: blood and fire and pillars of smoke. The sun shall be turned into darkness, and the moon into blood, before the coming of the great and awesome day of the Lord." Joel 2:28-31.*

This prophecy pictures the darkening of the sun and the moon into blood, as following the **OUTPOURING OF THE HOLY SPIRIT** and **WONDERS IN HEAVEN & EARTH**, neither of which has yet happened. Look carefully at the sequence in which these events are to occur:
 [1] Outpouring of the Holy Spirit;
 [2] Wonders in the heavens and earth;
 [3] Sun darkened and moon into blood (Dark Day);
 [4] The coming of the Lord.
This gives us a clear clue that this prophecy has a second occurrence that is still in our immediate future.

A Future Falling of the Stars

5. In connection with the falling of the stars, what would happen to the heavens?

> *"All the host of heaven shall be dissolved, and the heavens shall be rolled up like a scroll; all their host shall fall down as the leaf falls from the vine, and as fruit falling from a fig tree." Isaiah 34:4.*

Isaiah is shown in vision **THE HEAVENS ROLLED UP LIKE A SCROLL**, when the stars fall. The Bible refers to this in Revelation 6:14: "Then the sky receded as a scroll when it is rolled up." Isaiah makes it clearer that these two events will happen simultaneously. The splitting open of the heavens now allows all to view some threatening activity going on from inside that opening in the heavens. A violent attack from outer space is underway. This terrifying moment is where Chapter 6 leaves off, and Chapter 19, the explanatory chapter for the sixth seal, takes up the account.

Seal	Explanation
1 – White Horse	Chapter 7
2 – Red Horse	Chapters 8-11
3 – Black Horse	Chapters 12-14
4 – Pale Horse	Chapters 15 & 16
5 – Praying Martyrs	Chapters 17 & 18
6 – Second Coming	Chapter 19

Invasion From Outer Space

6. Who first appears from this opening in the sky?

"Now I saw heaven opened, and behold, a white horse. And He who sat on him was called Faithful and True, and in righteousness He judges and makes war. His eyes were like a flame of fire, and on His head were many crowns. He had a name written that no one knew except Himself. He was clothed with a robe dipped in blood, and His name is called The Word of God." Revelation 19:11-13.

The splitting open of the heavens reveals that threatening activity is on its way to planet earth. Out of this gaping hole in the heavens appears **CHRIST RIDING A WHITE HORSE.** There is no mistake about the identity of this majestic Being. In verse 16 He is called the King of Kings and Lord of Lords. He is coming to take control of this world.

7. Who accompany Him?

"And the armies in heaven, clothed in fine linen, white and clean, followed Him on white horses." Revelation 19:14.

No peaceful hand over of this earth to Christ will take place. No negotiations are suggested by either side. Christ returns to this earth prepared for a big battle. It will be the "battle of that great day of God Almighty." He shows up with **THE ARMIES OF HEAVEN,** expecting resistance and is prepared for it.

8. **What will the armies of earth do?**

   "And I saw the beast, the kings of the earth, and their armies, gathered together to make war against Him who sat on the horse and against His army." Revelation 19:17, 18.

Instead of welcoming Christ with songs of praise, instead of falling down in full surrender and yielding to this divine King of Kings, the rebellious armies of earth **MAKE WAR AGAINST CHRIST AND HIS ARMY**.

The inhabitants of earth view this as an unwelcome intrusion into their planet. They take up battle stations to challenge the invasion, hurling all the weaponry of modern warfare against these intruders from outer space. What a shame that the long-awaited return of Christ to earth has to be marred by the ugliness of war! Sinners refuse to yield their lives to the King of Kings, and they do not intend to yield their world to Him either.

9. **Who will be the battle's casualties?**

   "Then I saw an angel standing in the sun; and he cried with a loud voice, saying to all the birds that fly in the midst of heaven, Come and gather together for the supper of the great God, that you may eat the flesh of kings, the flesh of captains, the flesh of mighty men, the flesh of horses and of those who sit on them, and the flesh of all people, free and slave, both small and great." Revelation 19:17, 18.

Heaven announces its intent before the fighting begins. It is declared that no prisoners will be taken. No surrender will be accepted. It will be a fight to the death for all who participate in this opposition force from earth. When they see that their sophisticated weapons are powerless to turn back the angelic invasion, they will run for cover (see Revelation 6:15-17) to the mountains and caves, but none will escape. **ALL PEOPLE SMALL AND GREAT** will end up slain on the battle field of this earth.

Survivors

10. **What will Christ's army do first?**

    "Immediately after the tribulation of those days the sun will be darkened, and the moon will not give its light; the stars will fall

from heaven, and the power of the heavens will be shaken. Then the sign of the Son of Man will appear in heaven, and then all the tribes of the earth will mourn, and they will see the Son of Man coming on the clouds of heaven with power and great glory. And He will send His angels with a great sound of a trumpet, and they will gather together His elect from the four winds, from one end of heaven to the other." Matthew 24:29-31.

The main job of the angels is not to do battle with the opposition forces of earth. Jesus Himself will take care of that (Revelation 19:15, 21). The angels' main task is to swoop into the chaos and confusion and **GATHER TOGETHER ALL BELIEVERS**, taking them swiftly out of harm's way. These angel soldiers are heaven's Navy Seals Team 6. How this will all be done is the subject of our next lesson.

QUIZ FOR LESSON NO. 16

List any five supernatural events that will occur just prior to the arrival of Christ back to our earth. You do not need to list them in any particular order.

The Survivors
Lesson No. 17

Any Survivors?

The sixth seal, as well as its explanatory passage in Chapter 19, picture only the reaction of those who resist Christ at His second coming. If read alone, one might get the impression that no one survives. But this is only a partial account of what happens to people on the day Christ returns.

1.   What will happen to all who resist Christ's arrival?

   "Then the beast was captured, and with him the false prophet who worked signs in his presence, by which he deceived those who received the mark of the beast and those who worshiped his image. These two were cast alive into the lake of fire burning with brimstone. And the rest were killed with the sword which proceeded from the mouth of Him who sat on the horse. And all the birds were filled with their flesh." Revelation 19:20, 21.

It is plain that all who are unsaved when Christ arrives will not survive. They will all be **KILLED**. This Scripture gives the impression of global genocide, but it is only a partial account of the results of Christ's second coming.

2.   What two groups will be impacted by Christ's arrival?

   "Saying, We give You thanks, O Lord God Almighty, the One who is and who was and who is to come, because You have taken Your great power and reigned. The nations were angry, and Your wrath has come, and the time of the dead, that they should be judged, and that You should reward Your servants the prophets and the saints, and those who fear Your name, small and great, and should destroy those who destroy the earth." Revelation 11:17,18.

Both believers and unbelievers will be dealt with on the same day. **THE SAINTS** will be rewarded, and **THOSE DESTROYING THE EARTH** will be destroyed. All Christians once believed that the world would end as pictured here in Revelation --- both the saved and the unsaved are dealt with on the same day, when Christ comes the second time. Howev-

er, this is no longer the opinion of a majority of Christians today.
In recent years a new, innovative idea has been proposed and has received widespread acceptance among Christians. It is the suggestion that the rapture of the saints from this world does not occur simultaneously with, but precedes by seven years, the second coming of Christ. The new belief teaches that removal of the believers at the rapture will be done silently and secretly, with the unsaved totally unaware of it until after it has occurred. This concept is referred to as the "secret rapture," and all attempts to use this theory to interpret the book of Revelation have led to radical and unscriptural conclusions.

Fortunately, the rapture event is often mentioned in Scripture. Examining some of these passages will clear up in our minds any confusion caused by this rather modern theory.

Will the Unsaved Notice the Rapture?

3. What will be the reaction of the unsaved?

"Then the sign of the Son of Man will appear in heaven, and then all the tribes of the earth will mourn, and they will see the Son of Man coming on the clouds of heaven with power and great glory." Matthew 24:30.

The world will notice Christ's arrival, and many will **MOURN**. Their reaction indicates that they are unsaved. As Christ arrives to rapture the believers, the unsaved will be very aware of what is happening. The next verse describes the actual rapture of believers and gives us additional information about how it will be performed.

4. As the saved are raptured, what will be heard?

"And He will send His angels with a great sound of a trumpet, and they will gather together His elect from the four winds, from one end of heaven to the other." Matthew 24:31.

The Bible paints a very dramatic picture of Christ returning for His people. He is not pictured as stealing into this world unobserved, then sneaking His faithful followers, dead or alive, away from the earth.

Christ has nothing to be ashamed of and certainly will have no reason to avoid the unsaved noticing Him. His return for His faithful ones will be a very public and powerful event. On that day the angels will do their work of gathering and rapturing the believers with **A GREAT SOUND OF A TRUMPET.**

5. At the rapture, what sounds will be heard?

> *"For the Lord Himself will descend from heaven with a shout, with the trumpet of God. And the dead in Christ will rise first. Then we who are alive and remain shall be caught up together with them in the clouds to meet the Lord in the air. And thus we shall always be with the Lord. Therefore comfort one another with these words."* I Thessalonians 4:16-18.

This rescue of believers will be done with a **SHOUT, VOICE, AND TRUMPET.** This is often called the noisiest text in the Bible. The sound will soar to unbearable levels for the unbelievers. It will be impossible for anyone alive to be unaware of what is going on.

Will the Unsaved Survive the Event?

6. When the Lord comes "as a thief in the night," what are the results to this planet?

> *"But the day of the Lord will come as a thief in the night, in which the heavens will pass away with a great noise, and the elements will melt with fervent heat; both the earth and the works that are in it will be burned up. Therefore, since all these things will be dissolved, what manner of persons ought you to be in holy conduct and godliness, looking for and hastening the coming of the day of God, because of which the heavens will be dissolved, being on fire, and the elements will melt with fervent heat?"* II Peter 3:10-12.

The complete destruction of earth's environment renders this planet unable to sustain human, animal, or even plant life. The heavens **WILL PASS AWAY WITH A GREAT NOISE.** The elements **WILL MELT WITH FERVENT HEAT**. The works on the earth **WILL BE BURNED UP**.

The comparison to "a thief in the night" denotes the *"surprise"* of the event, not the *"quietness"* of it. It is clear that after Christ leaves with His raptured believers, this planet will be unfit for anyone to survive at all.

7. **What did Noah's flood do to the unsaved?**

   "And as it was in the days of Noah, so it will be also in the days of the Son of Man: they ate, they drank, they married wives, they were given in marriage, until the day that Noah entered the ark, and the flood came and destroyed them all." Luke 17:26, 27.

God removed the righteous ones by shutting them up in a specially constructed boat. When the flood came, not one person outside that boat survived. The flood **DESTROYED THEM ALL**.

8. **What did the fire do to the unsaved of Sodom?**

   "Likewise as it was also in the days of Lot: they ate, they drank, they bought, they sold, they planted, they built; but on the day that Lot went out of Sodom it rained fire and brimstone from heaven and destroyed them all." Luke 17:26, 27.

None of those left behind in Sodom escaped. The fire that came **DESTROYED THEM ALL**. One point often emphasized by Jesus about His second coming was the finality of it, for unbelievers and believers alike. The unsaved will not continue life as usual, making a little adjustment for the disappearance of so many.

The World Left Behind

9. **What will happen to those not taken in the rapture?**

   "I tell you, in that night there will be two men in one bed: the one will be taken and the other will be left. Two women will be grinding together: the one will be taken and the other left. Two men will be in the field: the one will be taken and the other left." Luke 17:34-36.

Many do not read this passage of Scripture carefully. They often think it says a lot more than it actually does. Nowhere in these texts does it state that the one left behind in the bed goes on sleeping until morning; or that the woman left behind at the grinding wheel goes on grinding day in and day out; or that the man left behind in the field will not notice his working partner ascending to the heavens. All that these texts say is that those who are not taken **WILL BE LEFT**. It says nothing about what will happen to those left behind. Earlier in that chapter, Jesus made it emphatically clear that they will not survive. They will all be destroyed.

10. **What will happen to this earth someday?**

> *"I beheld the earth, and indeed it was without form, and void; and the heavens, they had no light. I beheld the mountains, and indeed they trembled, and all the hills moved back and forth. I beheld, and indeed there was no man, and all the birds of the heavens had fled. I beheld, and indeed the fruitful land was a wilderness, and all its cities were broken down at the presence of the Lord, by His fierce anger." Jeremiah 4:23-26.*

The prophet Jeremiah was given a very alarming picture of the complete ruination of the earth and its environment some day. The earth was **WITHOUT FORM AND VOID**; the heavens had **NO LIGHT**; the mountains **TREMBLED**; mankind had mysteriously disappeared, he saw **NO MAN**; the birds **FLED** (they disappeared); the fruitful places were a sheer **WILDERNESS**; and all cities were **BROKEN DOWN**.

It is apparent that such a situation has not yet been experienced on this planet and, when it comes, this planet will be uninhabitable.

11. **What caused this global destruction?**

> *"I beheld, and indeed the fruitful land was a wilderness, and all its cities were broken down at the presence of the Lord, by His fierce anger. For thus says the Lord: the whole land shall be desolate; yet I will not make a full end." Jeremiah 4:26, 27.*

Jeremiah is told that all this destruction was not caused by man himself, but by **THE LORD'S FIERCE ANGER**. Jeremiah leaves no doubt in our minds as to who is responsible. God added a significant postscript: "Yet I will not make a full end." God has big plans for our planet, and He reveals them in the remaining portions of the book of Revelation.

Headed Where?

12.   Where does Christ meet the saved believers?

> *"For the Lord Himself will descend from heaven with a shout, with the voice of an archangel, and with the trumpet of God. And the dead in Christ will rise first. Then we who are alive and remain shall be caught up together with them in the clouds to meet the Lord in the air. And thus we shall always be with the Lord."*
> *I Thessalonians 4:16, 17.*

Christ does not settle down on this earth with the saved believers at this time. Things would be too chaotic here. He does not even touch the surface of the earth. Remaining suspended in the clouds of heaven, He instructs his angels to collect all believers and bring them to Him **IN THE AIR**. This meeting place is just the initial point of contact for believers with Christ.

13.   Where will Christ take the saved believers?

> *"Let not your heart be troubled; you believe in God, believe also in Me. In My Father's house are many mansions; if it were not so, I would have told you. I go to prepare a place for you. And if I go and prepare a place for you, I will come again and receive you to myself; that where I am, there you may be also." John 14:1-3.*

The place in the air where all meet Christ is merely a staging area. Once all are collected, they leave there for another destination. In some distant place in the heavens, Christ and His Father have a permanent residence, and Christ assures us that there is plenty of room there for us also. He then escorts us into outer space to His heavenly place of residence **WHERE HE IS**. Revelation gives us a glimpse of that special place, and we will study about it in a later lesson.

14.   How long will we stay in heaven with Christ?

> *"Blessed and holy is he who has part in the first resurrection. Over such the second death has no power, but they shall be priests of God and of Christ, and shall reign with Him a thousand years." Revelation 20:6.*

We will be guests of God and Christ for **A THOUSAND YEARS**. Heaven is not to be our permanent homeland. We are there for a vacation, not forever. What awaits us there and what will happen when we return to our home planet will be studied in our next lesson.

There are circulating today so many confusing teachings among Christians concerning the second coming of Christ. It would be helpful for us to compare and contrast the true teaching of the Bible with the popular understandings of today. This will aid us in separating truth from error and give us a clearer picture of what we can expect in the future when Christ comes for us.

PUBLIC, OR SECRET EVENT?

Popular Concept: The rapture will be a secret and silent event. Only believing Christians will see Christ appearing in the clouds of heaven. They will suddenly disappear, and the unbelievers will be mystified, totally unaware of what happened until after the event has taken place.

Bible Teaching: The rescue of believers from this world will be performed by Christ and His holy angels with the most dramatic display of power and glory ever witnessed by both believers and unbelievers.

> *"Then the sign of the Son of Man will appear in heaven, and then all the tribes of the earth will mourn, and they will see the Son of Man coming on the clouds of heaven with power and great glory. And He will send His angels with a great sound of a trumpet, and they will gather together His elect from the four winds, from one end of heaven to the other." Matthew 24:30, 31.*

The rapture will be very public and open to the view of unbelievers and believers alike.

BEFORE, OR AT THE SECOND COMING?

Popular Concept: The rapture will take place seven years before the coming of Christ. In other words, the rapture and the second coming of Christ are two different events which are separated by seven years.

Bible Teaching: The Bible consistently pictures these events as one. The rapture and the glorious second coming of Christ will occur together --- all part of one grand, glorious and climactic event.

"Now, brethren, concerning the coming of our Lord Jesus Christ and our gathering together to Him . . ." II Thessalonians 2:1.

Notice that the order given for these two events is exactly opposite of the popular theory today, which places our gathering together to meet him *"before,"* rather than *"after,"* the coming of Christ. In Paul's thinking they were all one event, happening simultaneously.

AT THE RAPTURE WILL UNBELIEVERS SURVIVE, OR DIE?

Popular Concept: A very prominent feature of today's misconceptions about the rapture is that all who are unprepared to go up in the rapture will be unharmed by it. They will go on living as usual, merely making some adjustments for the absence of the believers who had mysteriously disappeared.

Bible Teaching: The Bible emphatically teaches that all the wicked will be destroyed when the Lord returns, leaving the earth completely unpopulated.

". . . and to give you who are troubled rest with us when the Lord Jesus is revealed from heaven with His mighty angels, in flaming fire taking vengeance on those who do not know God, and on those who do not obey the gospel of our Lord Jesus Christ. These shall be punished with everlasting destruction from the presence of the Lord and from the glory of His power, when He comes, in that Day, to be glorified in His saints and to be admired among all those who believe." II Thessalonians 1:7-10.

AFTER THE RAPTURE WILL UNBELIEVERS HAVE A SECOND CHANCE, OR NO CHANCE, TO BE SAVED?

Popular Concept: It is maintained that all the unbelievers who are not taken to heaven in the rapture will have a second chance to be saved during the following seven years. Some teach that after the seven years (during the millennium) the unrepentant will even have a third chance of being saved.

Bible Teaching: Since probationary time for human beings closes a short time before the second coming of Christ and, since all who are not raptured are destroyed by the brightness of Christ's appearance, there can be no second opportunity for the unrepentant to be saved.

"He who is unjust, let him be unjust still; he who is filthy, let him be filthy still; he who is righteous, let him be righteous still; he who is holy, let him be holy still. And behold, I am coming quickly, and My reward is with Me, to give to every one according to his work." Revelation 22:10, 11.

QUIZ FOR LESSON NO. 17

Choose One Answer:

1. The rapture is:
   (A) Before the tribulation
   (B) After the tribulation

2. The rapture is:
   (A) A change of life for unbelievers
   (B) The end of life for unbelievers

3. The rapture is:
   (A) A secret event
   (B) A public event

4. The rapture is:
   (A) Before the second coming
   (B) At the second coming

5. The earth is:
   (A) Partially unpopulated after the rapture
   (B) Completely unpopulated after the rapture

The Third Coming of Christ
Lesson No. 18

Three Visits

No. 1   Two thousand years ago planet earth was honored by a visit from the Son of God. At that time He came to a Bethlehem stable, alone and almost undetected. He stayed on this earth for only 33 years and then left, promising to return.

No. 2   The time of His next visit is approaching. How different that second visit will be! First, He will rescue all believers and take them out of harm's way. He will then engage in a violent confrontation with all the unsaved, resulting in their destruction, along with the world they had lived in. Once again Christ will leave the earth, this time taking with Him to heaven all believers.

No. 3   Still, this earth has not seen the last of Him. The book of Revelation teaches that He will visit this earth for the third time, but not until 1,000 years have passed. The events clustered around this future time period are what we will now study.

The 1,000 Years Begin

1.   What great event begins the 1,000 years?

   "But the rest of the dead did not live again until the thousand years were finished. This is the first resurrection. Blessed and holy is he who has part in the first resurrection. Over such the second death has no power, but they shall be priests of God and of Christ, and shall reign with Him a thousand years." Revelation 20:5, 6.

While this time prophecy gives no precise date when it will begin, it does give us a well-known event which we can use as its starting point. **THE FIRST RESURRECTION** starts the heavenly time clock which keeps track of the time for 1,000 years.

2.   What is the first thing to happen when Jesus returns?

> *"For this we say to you by the word of the Lord, that we who are alive and remain until the coming of the Lord will by no means precede those who are asleep. For the Lord Himself will descend from heaven with a shout, with the voice of an archangel, and with the trumpet of God. And the dead in Christ will rise first. Then we who are alive and remain shall be caught up together with them in the clouds to meet the Lord in the air. And thus we shall always be with the Lord."* I Thessalonians 4:15-17.

When Jesus appears, the first thing on His mind are the dead believers. **THE DEAD IN CHRIST WILL RISE** from their graves, and join the living believers to meet Christ in the air. The resurrection and the rapture are on the same day Christ appears the second time. This is also the very day the 1,000 years begin.

3.   How many resurrections did Jesus mention?

> *"Do not marvel at this; for the hour is coming in which all who are in the graves will hear His voice and come forth --- those who have done good, to the resurrection of life, and those who have done evil, to the resurrection of condemnation."* John 5:28, 29.

Jesus identified **TWO** distinct resurrections and states that they differ by the kind of people who participate in them. In Revelation, He reveals that they are separated by 1,000 years!

4.   When will those who missed the first resurrection be raised?

> *"But the rest of the dead did not live again until the thousand years were finished. This is the first resurrection"* Revelation 20:5.

The phrase, "this is the first resurrection," is referring to the resurrection mentioned in the previous verse and expanded upon in verse 6. Only those who participate in the first resurrection are the "blessed" ones. The rest of the dead (those who are unsaved) will be raised **AFTER THE THOUSAND YEARS**.

5. What will happen to all who are not saved at the second coming of Christ?

> *". . . and to give you who are troubled rest with us when the Lord Jesus is revealed from heaven with His mighty angels. In flaming fire taking vengeance on those who do not know God, and on those who do not obey the gospel of our Lord Jesus Christ. These shall be punished with everlasting destruction from the presence of the Lord and from the glory of His power, when He comes, in that Day, to be glorified in His saints and to be admired among all those who believe, because our testimony among you was believed."* II Thessalonians 1:7-10.

The unbelievers alive at that time are destroyed. They will experience **DESTRUCTION**, not a minor change of lifestyle. The unbelievers who died before Christ returns remain in their graves until the end of the 1,000 years. Revelation will explain to us why all these unbelievers are brought back to life, even though they will not be saved.

During the 1,000 Years

6. When the Lord shuts up all sinners in a prison, when will He release them to be punished?

> *"The earth is violently broken, the earth is split open, the earth is shaken exceedingly. The earth shall reel to and fro like a drunkard, and shall totter like a hut; its transgression shall be heavy upon it, and it will fall, and not rise again. It shall come to pass in that day that the Lord will punish on high the host of exalted ones, and on the earth the kings of the earth. They will be gathered together, as prisoners are gathered in the pit, and will be shut up in the prison; after many days they will be punished."* Isaiah 24:19-22.

Sinners will not be free to enjoy this planet during those 1,000 years, because it is rendered uninhabitable for humans. All sinners are secured in the prison house of death, awaiting a release which Revelation will describe for us.

AFTER MANY DAYS these sinners will be brought forth for punishment. God did not reveal to the prophet Isaiah exactly how many days they would be imprisoned, but Revelation reveals to us that information: "the rest of the dead lived not again until the 1,000 years were finished."

7. Who else is imprisoned during the 1,000 years?

> *"Then I saw an angel coming down from heaven, having the key to the bottomless pit and a great chain in his hand. He laid hold of the dragon, that serpent of old, who is the Devil and Satan, and bound him for a thousand years; and he cast him into the bottomless pit, and shut him up, and set a seal on him, so that he should deceive the nations no more till the thousand years were finished. But after these things he must be released for a little while." Revelation 20:1-3.*

SATAN is also imprisoned during those 1,000 years. Instead of being in the prison house of death with all other sinners, he is imprisoned on this earth and kept alive.

Some have wondered why this chief of sinners gets to remain alive, while all other sinners are dead. This is because solitary confinement is worse than death. Satan will be bound to this dark and desolate earth, unable to talk to the saints in heaven. Neither can he communicate with unbelievers on earth, for they are all dead and unconscious. To this intensely active Devil the 1,000-year prison term will be intense torture, not a restful vacation.

Now let us switch our attention from Satan and his followers to see what is happening to Christ's followers during these 1,000 years.

8. Where does Christ take us at the rapture?

> *"Let not your heart be troubled; you believe in God, believe also in Me. In My Father's house are many mansions, if it were not so, I would have told you. I go to prepare a place for you. And if I go and prepare a place for you, I will come again and receive you to Myself; that where I am, there you may be also." John 14:1-3.*

Christ does not come to live in our world with us. He takes us to live in His world with Him **WHERE HE IS**. There will be no peace and prosperity on earth during this lengthy period of time. We believers will be living in peace and prosperity during those 1,000 years, but in heaven, not on this earth, as some teach today. The Bible not only tells us where the believers will be during that long period, but also what they will be doing.

9. **In what two tasks will believers be engaged?**
"And I saw thrones, and they sat on them, and judgment was committed to them. Then I saw the souls of those who had been beheaded for their witness to Jesus and for the word of God, who had not worshiped the beast or his image, and had not received his mark on their foreheads or on their hands. And they lived and reigned with Christ for a thousand years." Revelation 20:4.

Those will be very busy days for the saved saints. They will have administrative duties as they **REIGN WITH CHRIST** over the vast universe outside our world. They will also have judiciary duties as they engage in a work of **JUDGMENT**. We will study more about that in a future lesson.

Ending of the 1,000 Years

10. **What happens to Satan when the 1,000 years expire?**

"Now when the thousand years have expired, Satan will be released from his prison." Revelation 20:7.

His solitary confinement terminates with the resurrection of all the wicked. He is thus **RELEASED FROM HIS PRISON**.

11. **When released, what will he do?**

". . . and will go out to deceive the nations which are in the four corners of the earth, Gog and Magog, to gather them together to battle, whose number is as the sand of the sea." Revelation 20:8.

It is after the wicked are raised to life by Christ that Satan goes about his old work to **DECEIVE THE NATIONS**.

12. What will happen to those who were dead during the 1,000 years?

> *"But the rest of the dead did not live again until the thousand years were finished." Revelation 20:5.*

Once more this world is filled with wicked people. Every one of them were dead during the 1,000 years, but at its end they **LIVE AGAIN**. Satan is freed from his solitary confinement by the presence of people. The second resurrection has taken place---"the resurrection of damnation.'

13. What is the military target in his battle plans?

> *"They went up on the breadth of the earth and surrounded the camp of the saints and the beloved city." Revelation 20:9.*

The appearance of a dazzling **CITY** on the broken and devastated earth would naturally get the attention of all who are on the outside. John refers to it as the **CAMP OF THE SAINTS**. It is not an empty city because God's people are inside. The city is no longer in heaven, for Satan's armies had to travel over "the breadth of the earth" to surround it. Later, John mentioned that he had seen it in vision descending from heaven to earth.

14. Who are inside that city?

> *"Then I, John, saw the holy city New Jerusalem, coming down out of heaven from God, prepared as a bride adorned for her husband. And I heard a loud voice from heaven saying, Behold, the tabernacle of God is with men, and He will dwell with them, and they shall be His people. God Himself will be with them and be their God." Revelation 21:2, 3.*

GOD AND HIS PEOPLE are safe inside that city. It apparently arrived just before the Lord resurrects the wicked dead of all ages, loosing Satan from his solitary imprisonment. When Satan and his army of unbelievers arrive around that city, it will be the first and last time the entire human race will be together face-to-face.

15. How long will Satan have to deceive everyone?

> *". . .and he cast him into the bottomless pit, and shut him up, and set a seal on him, so that he should deceive the nations no more*

till the thousand years were finished. But after these things he must be released for a little while." Revelation 20:3.

These now-resurrected unbelievers are given **A LITTLE WHILE** to live once again. This period is of an unknown, but short duration. During this time Satan's work will be intense, and all the resurrected sinners will be very vulnerable to deception. These people will have no idea who brought them back to life, and Satan will naturally take the credit for it. He now asks them to engage with him in a battle against God and the New Jerusalem inhabitants. He assures these deluded people that he has the power to restore them to life once again in the future if they become casualties in this war.

16. **What is the final fate of this rebel army?**

   "And fire came down from God out of heaven and devoured them" Revelation 20:9.

As we shall see in a future lesson, there will be no battle taking place. Before the rebel army can muster a coordinated attack, **FIRE FROM GOD DEVOURS THEM**. But, according to Revelation, a very unusual scene will take place even before that happens. It is symbolized by the seventh seal, and this will be the subject of our next lesson.

QUIZ FOR LESSON NO. 18

Choose One:

1. One thing that happens at the BEGINNING of the 1,000 years.
   (A) The third coming of Christ
   (B) The second coming of Christ
   (C) The first coming of Christ

2. Another thing that happens at the BEGINNING of the 1,000 years.
   (A) New Jerusalem descends from heaven
   (B) Nothing unusual
   (C) Rapture of all believers

3. One thing that happens DURING the 1,000 years.
   (A) Saints judge unbelievers
   (B) Unbelievers have a second chance to be saved
   (C) Satan released from his prison

4. One thing that happens at the END of the 1,000 years.
   (A) The first resurrection (believers)
   (B) The second resurrection (unbelievers)
   (C) No resurrection at all

5. Another thing that happens at the END of the 1,000 years.
   (A) Satan chained and imprisoned
   (B) Satan released from his prison
   (C) Satan deceives the nations

A Solemn Silence
Lesson No. 19

The Seventh Seal

We have concluded the study of the sixth seal and are now ready for the seventh. Over 1,000 years have passed since that sixth seal opened with a spectacular display of supernatural events in the heavens that quickly culminated in the arrival of Christ. This last seal is separated from the other six, because it deals with an event that is far removed from the time of the end that preceded the coming of Christ, yet it is very much related to it.

The Last Seal

1. What occurred throughout heaven?

   "When He opened the seventh seal, there was silence in heaven for about half an hour." Revelation 8:1.

The breaking open of the last seal exposes the contents of that book. The entire universe is spellbound, and **SILENCE** pervades the heavens.

2. How long did this silence last?

   "When He opened the seventh seal, there was silence in heaven for about half an hour." Revelation 8:1.

Just **HALF-AN-HOUR** was involved in this seal event. This is the shortest time prophecy in the Bible, and we must not be misled by the shortness of the time. These moments are the most solemn moments in the history of this world and God's universe. To understand the reason for this profound silence, we must turn to Revelation's explanation later on in the book.

Seal	Explanation
1 – White Horse	Chapter 7
2 – Red Horse	Chapters 8-11
3 – Black Horse	Chapters 12-14
4 – Pale Horse	Chapters 15 & 16
5 – Praying Martyrs	Chapters 17 & 18
6 – Second Coming	Chapter 19
7 – Silence	Chapter 20

The Final Judgment

3. At the end of the 1,000 years, what did John see before the unbelievers are destroyed?

> *"Then I saw a great white throne and Him who sat on it, from whose face the earth and the heaven fled away. And there was found no place for them." Revelation 20:11.*

In the vision there comes into John's view **GOD ON A GREAT WHITE THRONE.** This is called the Great White Throne Judgment. It is also known as the post-millennial judgment, because it happens after ("post") the 1,000 years. It is called the "final" judgment, because there are other judgments before this. We will have a look at each of them before we are done with this lesson.

4. Who stood before this imposing throne?

> *"And I saw the dead, small and great, standing before God, and books were opened. And another book was opened, which is the Book of Life. And the dead were judged according to their works, by the things which were written in the books. The sea gave up the dead who were in it, and Death and Hades delivered up the dead who were in them. And they were judged, each one according to his works." Revelation 20:12, 13.*

THE DEAD, SMALL AND GREAT, were arraigned and judged by God on His throne. All of these people were in their graves, but came back to life after the 1,000 years ended (verse 5). All of them were unrepentant sinners from our world, along with Satan and his host of fallen angels. God is about to put sin completely out of His universe, and the execution of all sinners is moments away. The seriousness and solemnity of this event is difficult to describe. Before God does so, He wants all these condemned beings to understand why. Keep in mind that all of this is going on no where else but upon this earth, and all heavenly beings are looking on as witnesses.

5. When God reveals the guilt of sinners, what will be their response?

> *"Now we know that whatever the law says, it says to those who are under the law, that every mouth may be stopped, and all the world may become guilty before God." Romans 3:19.*

When **EVERY MOUTH WILL BE STOPPED**, silence will result. Silence is the dominant characteristic of any courtroom. When a serious trial is in progress, no unrelated or frivolous conversation is engaged in by those on trial; not even by visitors watching the proceedings. This judgment scene will be the most serious of all judgment scenes, and will be characterized by a quietness so deep it will be painful to all.

6.   What is used as evidence at this time?

"And I saw the dead, small and great, standing before God, and books were opened. And another book was opened, which is the Book of Life. And the dead were judged according to their works, by the things which were written in the books." Revelation 20:12.

These "**BOOKS**" evidently have video, as well as audio, capabilities. For all the lost it will be a most painful silence, as each is shown their individual part in rejecting God and His plan of redemption for them.

7.   How long will this judgment proceeding last?

"When He opened the seventh seal, there was silence in heaven for about half an hour." Revelation 8:1.

ABOUT HALF-AN-HOUR is an interesting expression. The adjective describing this half-hour is significant. "About" means approximately. This is a clear clue that this time period is not symbolic, but literal, for all prophetic time periods that are symbolic are extremely precise. Never is the adjective "about" used in describing them.

In just 30 painful minutes the shameful history of the world and each one's participation in it will pass before their view. With more precision than the most state-of-the-art recording device today, heaven's books will be opened and all will have their lives replayed before them. The accuracy of this rapid replay will extend down to every word, thought, and motive. Argument and denial will be impossible

The book of Revelation predicts not one, but three judgments of man by God. This one is the last, or final one. Let's take a look at the judgment to take place just prior to this one.

Another Judgment

8. During the 1,000 years, what special work will be assigned to those who are saved?

   "And I saw thrones, and they sat on them, and judgment was committed to them." Revelation 20:4.

This **JUDGMENT** will occur in heaven, not on this earth, as the final one is. It will last a full 1,000 years, in contrast to the Great White Throne Judgment which will only take about half-an-hour. When in heaven, the believers will be invited by Christ to review the records of all who are lost. The reason for this is not to decide who will be saved, or lost. That has already been decided in another judgment before this one. It is the degree of punishment that must be decided in this phase of God's judgment process. Having the saved saints assist in such decisions will give them full opportunity to see how just God was with the unsaved. It will satisfy all their questions as to why certain loved ones were not saved. It will also prepare them to accept the upcoming execution of the lost in the lake of fire at the end of the 1,000 years.

9. What two groups will be judged by the saints?

   "Dare any of you, having a matter against another, go to law before the unrighteous, and not before the saints? Do you not know that the saints will judge the world? And if the world will be judged by you, are you unworthy to judge the smallest matters? Do you not know that we shall judge angels? How much more things that pertain to this life?" I Corinthians 6:1-3.

The apostle Paul was referring to this millennial judgment, when he revealed that saved human beings will judge **THE WORLD AND ANGELS**. It is the only one of God's three phases of judgment in which man takes a judicial part.

The saints will be capable of making good decisions during that heavenly tribunal, because the books containing every detail of an individual's life, both man and angel, will be available. Decisions will not be influenced by relationships, but by the cold, hard facts.

10. Will all sinners receive the same amount of punishment?

> *"And that servant who knew his master's will, and did not prepare himself or do according to his will, shall be beaten with many stripes. But he who did not know, yet committed things deserving of stripes, shall be beaten with few. For everyone to whom much is given, from him much will be required; and to whom much has been committed, of him they will ask the more." Luke 12:47, 48.*

The answer is clearly **NO**. It is a fundamental principle of justice that "the punishment must fit the crime." When it comes to bringing violators of the law to justice, there is no such thing as "one size fits all."

Jesus taught that all sinners will not receive the identical punishment. That would not be fair and just. The book of Revelation says that each will be "judged according to their works." This makes necessary a weighing of each person's deeds and coming to some agreement as to how guilty a person is. God asks His saved people to help Him judge what that penalty will be for each person who is lost.

The book of Revelation speaks of yet another judgment—a third one. It is actually the first one to occur. (We are working backwards in our study of the judgments.)

Still Another Judgment

11. While the final gospel message is spreading worldwide, what is announced about God's judgment?

> *"Then I saw another angel flying in the midst of heaven, having the everlasting gospel to preach to those who dwell on the earth---to every nation, tribe, tongue, and people---saying with a loud voice, Fear God and give glory to Him, for the hour of His judgment has come; and worship Him who made heaven and earth, the sea and springs of water." Revelation 14:6, 7.*

It is apparently before the close of human probation that this "gospel" message is given to the world, alerting people that **THE HOUR OF HIS JUDGMENT HAS COME**.

Not "will" come, but "has" come, announces this angel. Here is brought to view the fact that God will be involved in some type of judgment before the close of human probation, while the gospel message is still being preached during the time of the end. It is the first of the three phases of God's judgment. This phase is conducted in heaven by God Himself before Jesus returns, and it is often referred to as the "pre-millennial" judgment.

12.   What does Jesus have with Him when He returns to earth?

"And behold, I am coming quickly, and My reward is with Me, to give to every one according to his work." Revelation 22:12.

THE REWARD FOR EVERYONE is with Christ when He returns. This means that before He even shows up here in the clouds of heaven, His decision, or judgment, has been made with regard to everyone's fate.

Many have the erroneous belief that when Jesus returns He will set up some type of judgment proceeding, deciding at that moment who are saved and who are not. This text makes it clear, however, that when He returns He has already made that decision, bringing His reward with Him.

13.   In a vision, what did Daniel witness God begin?

"I watched till thrones were put in place, and the Ancient of Days was seated; His garment was white as snow, and the hair of His head was like pure wool. His throne was a fiery flame, its wheels a burning fire; a fiery stream issued and came forth from before Him. A thousand thousands ministered to Him; ten thousand times ten thousand stood before Him. The court was seated, and the books were opened." Daniel 7:9, 10.

A COURT SESSION is witnessed by Daniel in vision. Daniel saw into the future from his day to the time when God would begin this work of judgment. Notice that it occurs in heaven, not on this earth. An earlier vision given to Daniel revealed that the opening of this heavenly court would be 2300 years from his time, a prediction that identifies 1844 as the precise year it would take place (see Daniel 8, 9).

This is the judgment that is going on when that angel of Revelation 14 alerts earth's inhabitants that "the hour of His judgment has come." It is often called the "investigative judgment," because it is in this judgment that God decides who is saved and who is lost. He will later confirm and defend His decision with the saved saints in heaven during the 1,000 years, enlisting the saints' help in determining how guilty each condemned person is. Then at the end of the 1,000 years God will show each sinner the reasons for the punishment, revisiting their lives with them in fast motion, so that no one will accuse God of being unjust in the punishment and extermination of all unrepentant sinners.

14.   For what did the apostle Paul say God has pre-set a time?

"Truly, these times of ignorance God overlooked, but now commands all men everywhere to repent, because He has appointed a day on which He will judge the world in righteousness by the Man whom He has ordained. He has given assurance of this to all by raising Him from the dead." Acts 17:30, 31.

Paul reveals to us that God has established the time **WHEN HE WILL JUDGE THE WORLD** and that it was already pre-set. We have discovered in our study that the book of Revelation reveals that God's judgment will be performed in three distinct and separate stages:

[1]   The judgment in heaven before Christ's second coming will start the 1,000 years. Bible prophecy pinpoints it as starting in the year 1844, ending just before Christ's return when probation closes for all human beings. Revelation 14:6, 7

[2]   The judgment in heaven all during the 1,000 years will be when Christ will enlist the help of the saved saints to determine appropriate penalties. Revelation 20:4

[3]   The judgment on earth, called the Great White Judgment, will be when the results of the two previous judgments are opened to the condemned sinners just before their execution.

QUIZ FOR LESSON NO. 19

A. Before the 1,000 years
B. During the 1,000 years
C. After the 1,000 years

1. This judgment takes place in heaven.

2. During this judgment Christ will ask the saved to help Him arrive at a suitable punishment for each unsaved person.

3. This judgment takes place on this earth.

4. During this judgment all unbelievers are sentenced and punished on the same day.

5. During this judgment it is decided who will be saved and who will be lost.

The Lake of Fire
Lesson No. 20

The Ultimate Punishment

Before we begin our study let us think about the concept of punishment.

[1] There is embedded in the nature of human beings a sense of justice. We are naturally outraged if criminals are not held accountable for their mistreatment of others. All agree, except the criminals themselves, that wrongdoers must be "brought to justice."

[2] God has embedded in His nature the very same principle. It is even more pronounced in Him than in us. He is not only a God of love, but a just and righteous God. Because He is just, He can not excuse sinful behavior. He also cannot rest until wrong doers are brought to justice.

[3] How to administer justice is different with God than the methods man uses. Man uses money to punish criminals. Courts order fines or restitution to be paid to rectify some types of wrongdoing. Man also uses time to punish criminals. Depending upon the seriousness of a crime, the condemned must spend a certain amount of time incarcerated. But God cannot utilize either of these two methods of punishment, because at the second resurrection after the 1,000 years, the wicked have no money, and God cannot use time. It would mean rewarding evildoing with time which would be extending their life. The Bible says, "The wages of sin is death," not life.

[4] Therefore God has only one option open to Him to use as a tool for punishing evildoers. It is a tool that He can appropriately quantify and control, so that the punishment will fit each crime. It is pain, and that is what the lake of fire is all about. In the Bible it is called His "strange work," for He is a God of love as well as a God of justice, yet it is an absolute necessity.

1. **What will be the destiny of all unsaved people?**

   "And anyone not found written in the Book of Life was cast into the lake of fire." Revelation 20:15.

The concept of sinners being someday burned up by God is alluded to in the Old Testament, but is very prominent in Jesus' teachings and in the book of Revelation. There are many questions about this possibility, and Revelation will provide answers. **THE LAKE OF FIRE** pictured in Revelation is in complete harmony with other Scriptures that mention it. Putting all these references together we can get a picture of when, where, and how this burning will take place.

When?

2. **When will this burning of sinners take place?**

    "Therefore as the tares are gathered and burned in the fire, so it will be at the end of this age. The Son of Man will send out His angels, and they will gather out of His kingdom all things that offend, and those who practice lawlessness, and will cast them into the furnace of fire. There will be wailing and gnashing of teeth." Matthew 13:40-42.

Many are taught to believe that this hell fire is currently burning somewhere, receiving its victims one by one at their death. Jesus clears up this misconception. He says that all sinners receive this punishment together, **AT THE END OF TIME**.

3. **After what period of time will this fire burn?**

    "Now when the thousand years have expired, Satan will be released from his prison and will go out to deceive the nations which are in the four corners of the earth, Gog and Magog, to gather them together to battle, whose number is as the sand of the sea. They went up on the breadth of the earth and surrounded the camp of the saints and the beloved city. And fire came down from God out of heaven and devoured them. The devil, who deceived them, was cast into the lake of fire and brimstone where the beast and the false prophet are. And they will be tormented day and night forever and ever." Revelation 20:7-10.

Revelation agrees with Jesus' earlier statement that the burning fire was not ongoing while He was here on earth, but will take place at the end of time. Here in Revelation Jesus pinpoints the precise time: It will be ignited and do its work **AFTER THE 1,000 YEARS**.

If sinners were to begin burning immediately upon their death this would be a great travesty of justice. Millions would burn longer than others, not because they were greater sinners, but because they had the misfortune of living at an earlier time in history. Jesus is clear in His gospel teaching and in His Revelation description. Hell is not going on today, but is a future event.

Where?

4. Where will sinners, as well as believers, receive their reward?

   "If the righteous will be recompensed on the earth, how much more the ungodly and the sinner." Proverbs 11:31.

It will be **ON THE EARTH,** not down in some lower region, or off on another location in space, but right here on our planet.

5. Where will Satan receive his punishment?

   "You defiled your sanctuaries by the multitude of your iniquities, by the iniquity of your trading; therefore I brought fire from your midst; it devoured you, and I turned you to ashes upon the earth in the sight of all who saw you." Ezekiel 28:18.

This punishment will be meted out to Satan in plain sight of some onlookers. The execution will not be a private affair, but will be carried out in public, **UPON THE EARTH.**

6. What will the saved believers be able to do after the unsaved are burned up?

   "For behold, the day is coming, burning like an oven, and all the proud, yes, all who do wickedly will be stubble. And the day which is coming shall burn them up, says the Lord of hosts, that will leave them neither root nor branch. But to you who fear My name the Sun of Righteousness shall arise with healing in His wings; and you shall go out and grow fat like stall-fed calves. You shall trample the wicked, for they shall be ashes under the soles of your feet on the day that I do this, says the Lord of hosts." Malachi 4:1-3.

The Bible places the burning punishment on the surface of our earth where people can walk. This Scripture does not say that the wicked will be walked on while they are burning. When the burning is finished, the saved believers can **WALK ON THEIR ASHES**, at the very place where they were punished.

7. Where will the wicked be standing when this fire breaks upon them?

   "They went up on the breadth of the earth and surrounded the camp of the saints and the beloved city. And fire came down from God out of heaven and devoured them." Revelation 20:9.

They reached the city by walking on the surface of the earth, surrounding the New Jerusalem that had descended from heaven on the same spot where the old city of Jerusalem had been. Revelation pictures the wicked as standing **ON THE BREADTH OF THE EARTH**, at the time of the burning. The earth does not open to reveal a burning inferno. Hell fire drops down on the wicked; the wicked do not drop down into it.

Who Is In Charge?

8. When God planned the fires of hell, whom did He originally have in mind?

   "Then He will also say to those on the left hand, Depart from Me, you cursed, into the everlasting fire prepared for the devil and his angels." Matthew 25:41.

THE DEVIL AND HIS ANGELS will be in that final fire, along with all his followers. Satan is not the pitchfork supervisor of this burning inferno. He is its chief victim. The concept of him being the sinister tormentor in charge of the fire is a myth concocted by those who know little of what the Bible really teaches about hell.

9. How does Satan enter this fire?

   "The devil, who deceived them, was cast into the lake of fire and brimstone where the beast and the false prophet are. And they will be tormented day and night forever and ever." Revelation 20:10.

Clearly, the fire was not a comfortable place for him. **HE IS CAST INTO IT** and is as reluctant as any of us would be to end up there.

10. Who are really in charge of this hell fire?

"Then a third angel followed them, saying with a loud voice, If anyone worships the beast and his image, and receives his mark on his forehead or on his hand, he himself shall also drink of the wine of the wrath of God, which is poured out full strength into the cup of His indignation. He shall be tormented with fire and brimstone in the presence of the holy angels and in the presence of the Lamb." Revelation 14:9, 10.

Here are revealed the real supervisors of that inferno: **THE LAMB AND THE HOLY ANGELS.** God would never give Satan charge of such punishment, because he couldn't be trusted to be fair. However, it can be said of God, "true and righteous are Your judgments." Revelation 16:7.

11. After this burning is over, what is Satan's future?

"You defiled your sanctuaries by the multitude of your iniquities, by the iniquity of your trading; therefore I brought fire from your midst; it devoured you, and I turned you to ashes upon the earth in the sight of all who saw you. All who knew you among the peoples are astonished at you; you have become a horror, and shall be no more forever." Ezekiel 28:18, 19.

The Devil will not be punished in that fire for a time and then released to go on his way. The Lord promised, **HE SHALL BE NO MORE FOREVER.** There is no exit from that fire for anyone --- not even the mighty Devil himself.

What Will Burn?

In the minds of many, there is confusion about just what will be burned in the lake of fire. Those who teach that a sinner drops down into hell at the moment of death need to explain why he is still seen in his coffin at the funeral service. The reason most often given is that only a part of the sinner drops down into hell---his "soul," minus his body. Let us see if this reasoning stands up to the Bible's picture of hell.

12. What part of man will end up in hell?

"If your right eye causes you to sin, pluck it out and cast it from you; for it is more profitable for you that one of your members perish, than for your whole body to be cast into hell." Matthew 5:29.

Here is evidence that hell is not burning right now. Jesus says that when it does burn, **THE WHOLE BODY** will be in it. If the unsaved drop down into hell immediately at their death, why is their body still visible in the casket at their funeral?

13. What other part of man will end up in hell?

> *"And do not fear those who kill the body but cannot kill the soul. But rather fear Him who is able to destroy both soul and body in hell."* Matthew 10:28.

Jesus taught that everything about a man will be destroyed in that future hell: **HIS SOUL**, as well as his body. Jesus insists that everything about a person will be destroyed in that hell fire, not just a certain part.

14. What will happen to people before the fire engulfs them?

> *"But the rest of the dead did not live again until the thousand years were finished."* Revelation 20:5.

All who do not rise in the first resurrection at the beginning of the 1,000 years are destined for the lake of fire. However, before they are cast into that fire, **THEY WILL LIVE AGAIN**.

Jesus called this coming back to life, "the resurrection of condemnation." Every single human being that ends up in that burning fire will have first experienced a resurrection. By definition, "resurrection" is a return to bodily form, not to a spirit form.

15. How completely will the wicked be burned up?

> *"For behold, the day is coming, burning like an oven, and all the proud, yes, all who do wickedly will be stubble. And the day which is coming shall burn them up, says the Lord of hosts, that will leave them neither root nor branch."* Malachi 4:1.

"Up" is a very significant word. They will not be just "burned," but **BURNED UP**. Nothing about them will survive to bring back their existence.

How Long?

16. How long will the wicked be tormented?

"And they will be tormented day and night forever and ever." Revelation 20:10.

This text uses a familiar term to us: **FOREVER AND EVER**. It is a popular description of hell for most people. It confirms their belief that this hell fire will never end. But Jesus promised the "the meek shall inherit the earth." Does this mean that we have to watch this awful scene every day of our lives for all eternity? From this text alone, it would seem that the fire will never cease. But let us take a closer look at the verse just before this one.

17. What will the fire do to the wicked people?

"They went up on the breadth of the earth and surrounded the camp of the saints and the beloved city. And fire came down from God out of heaven and devoured them." Revelation 20:9.

They will be **DEVOURED**. The description in these two verses seems to be contradictory. How can a person be devoured, yet be tormented "forever?" The solution to this confusion is to understand what the Bible means by its use of the word "forever."

18. How long did Samuel's mother plan for her son to serve in the house of the Lord?

"But Hannah did not go up, for she said to her husband, Not until the child is weaned; then I will take him, that he may appear before the Lord and remain there forever.
"Therefore I also have lent him to the Lord; as long as he lives he shall be lent to the Lord." I Samuel 1:22, 28.

Here Hannah uses the term "forever" and later uses other words to explain what she meant when she said, "**AS LONG AS HE LIVES**."

The Bible does not use the word "forever" only in the sense in which we use it in these modern times. When the word "forever" is used with the verb "to live," it naturally means for all eternity. Otherwise, it means that the activity referred to will last as long as life exists. Never does the Bible say that the wicked will "live forever" in hell, or in any other place.

It says that they will be "tormented forever." They will be feeling the pain all the time they are alive in the flames. If, as we have learned, the life of Satan himself will end in hell and "never shall he be anymore," that would certainly be true of all the wicked as well.

BIBLE FACTS ABOUT HELL

The Bible gives a very different description of hell than is generally understood by so many today. Because the difference is so significant and, the misconception is so widespread, it would be helpful for us to summarize all the important facts the Bible gives us about this subject.

Future, Not Present

The Bible teaches that the fires of hell will not be ignited until after the 1,000 years, at the very end of this world's history.
The general teaching today is that the fires of hell are already burning and the unsaved fall down into it immediately upon their death.

"Therefore as the tares are gathered and burned in the fire, so it will be at the end of this age. The Son of Man will send out His angels and they will gather out of His kingdom all things that offend, and those who practice lawlessness, and will cast them into the furnace of fire." Matthew 13:40-42.

On the Ground, Not Under It

The Bible teaches that the place of the fire will be on the surface of the earth, in the area of the present old city of Jerusalem.
The general teaching today is that this fiery hell is located in some subterranean area deep beneath the earth's surface.

"They went up on the breadth of the earth and surrounded the camp of the saints and the beloved city. And fire came down from God out of heaven and devoured them." Revelation 20:9.

Body and Soul, Not Just the Soul

The Bible teaches that the whole person, body and soul, will be involved in that fiery hell.

The general teaching today is that only bodiless souls will be punished in hell.

"And do not fear those who kill the body but cannot kill the soul, but rather fear Him who is able to destroy both soul and body in hell." Matthew 10:28.

The Devil Is a Victim, Not the Supervisor

The Bible teaches that the Devil himself will be punished in the fiery hell.
The general teaching today is that the Devil is in charge of hell and supervises the torture with his pitchfork.

". . . I brought fire from your midst; it devoured you, and I turned you to ashes in the sight of all who saw you." Ezekiel 28:18.

Victims Burned to Ashes, Not Unendingly

The Bible teaches that after a period of torment, hell's victims will be reduced to ashes.
The general teaching today is that hell's victims will spend eternity in the fire.

"For behold, the day is coming, burning like an oven, and all the proud, yes, all who do wickedly will be stubble. And the day which is coming shall burn them up, says the Lord of hosts, that will leave them neither root nor branch." Malachi 4:1.

"Forever"

Revelation 14:11 and 20:10 use the word "forever" to describe the torment of all those in the lake of fire. Today, we use that word only to mean "unending," but the Bible uses it to mean "as long as life lasts." An example of this is Exodus 21:1-6, where a slave who decides to remain in the employ of his owner "will belong to his master forever." This explains why, in Revelation 20:10, the torment is forever and ever, yet in the verse before (verse 9), it states that they are "devoured." We must let the Bible tell us what it means, and not assign our own personal meaning to its words.

The Rich Man and Lazarus Parable

Almost all of today's misconceptions about the fiery hell are based upon a story Jesus told in Luke 16:19-13. If one takes this as a true-to-life account, it makes Jesus contradict not only the rest of Scripture, but even His own statements about hell. If one understands this to be a parable, then all the details are not necessarily literally true.

Before this, in Luke 16:1-12, Jesus told another parable about a wealthy man's manager who fraudulently manipulated the accounting books for personal benefit. Jesus then used the manager as an example for Christians to prepare for the future life. We should not conclude from this that Jesus taught that dishonesty is a proper way to prepare for eternal life.

In Judges 9:8-15 is a parable about trees talking together to decide who will be king among them. It is just a parable, and we should not conclude from this that the Bible teaches that trees can talk.

QUIZ FOR LESSON NO. 20

True or False?

1. Hell came into existence when the first sinner died.

2. Hell is situated deep below the surface of the earth.

3. God has given the Devil charge of hell.

4. The victims of hell will eventually be burned up completely.

5. There is no eternal life in hell.

A New World Order
Lesson No. 21

We are approaching the end of our study of Revelation's picture of end-time events. After using the Seven Churches prophecy to bridge the reader from John's day to that time of the end, the book has used the Seven Seals prophecy to give us thumbnail sketches of the seven most important events during that time. The remainder of the book devotes itself to amplifying those events with more background, details, and enhancements, dealing with them in the very same order. All of this ends with the complete annihilation of sin and sinners. Now, before the book closes, it gives us just a glimpse of what lies ahead in eternity.

Revelation's Final Chapters

1. **What new things does John now see?**

    "Now I saw a new heaven and a new earth, for the first heaven and the first earth had passed away. Also there was no more sea." Revelation 21:1.

There will be no return trip back to heaven. John sees a beautiful scene of **A NEW HEAVEN AND A NEW EARTH.** Earth's experience with sin is complete at the end of Chapter 20. The remaining two chapters focus on life when sin and sinners are a thing of the past.

The New City

2. **What is the first new thing John is shown?**

    "Then I, John, saw the holy city, New Jerusalem, coming down out of heaven from God, prepared as a bride adorned for her husband." Revelation 21:2.

The first and main attraction in this new environment is a city John identifies as a **NEW JERUSALEM**. Once it comes into John's view it captures his entire attention for the remainder of the book.

3. **Who are the occupants of this city?**

    "And I heard a loud voice from heaven saying, Behold, the tabernacle of God is with men, and He will dwell with them, and they shall be His people. God Himself will be with them and be their God." Revelation 211:3.

It is moving day for God. It will be a monumental change for Him. It will also drastically change the lifestyle of human beings. The fact that **GOD** is dwelling in the city means that **HIS PEOPLE** will be permanently around Him.

4.   **What type of lighting system will illuminate the city?**

> *"The city had no need of the sun or of the moon to shine in it, for the glory of God illuminated it. The Lamb is its light." Revelation 21:23.*

> *"There shall be no night there: they need no lamp nor light of the sun, for the Lord God gives them light. And they shall reign forever and ever." Revelation 22:5.*

The entire city (and it is a massive one) will be lit by **THE GLORY OF GOD**. The type of lighting system used for this new city will not be a created light such as the sun, or an artificial light such as a lamp. It will be the glorious light shining directly from God. It will never get dark inside the city, since the light emitting from God never dissipates.

One will need to go outside the city to experience darkness. When we speak of darkness we are speaking relatively. Isaiah 30:26 says that the sun outside the city will be seven times brighter than it is now and the light of the moon will be as bright as the sun is now. The intensity of darkness we now experience will be a relic of the old world we once lived in.

5.   **What is the basic shape of the city?**

> *"And he who talked with me had a gold reed to measure the city, its gates, and its wall. The city is laid out as a square; its length is as great as its breadth. And he measured the city with the reed: twelve thousand furlongs. Its length, breadth, and height are equal." Revelation 21:15, 16.*

The city is a brand new type of creation by God. It is built on the **SQUARE** principle, which employs right angles. In the Genesis creation the square principle is noticeably absent. All matter is formed on the curve principle. Our globe is round, and all features of the human body are curved or rounded. There are no square trees, flowers, birds, animals, rain drops or snow flakes.

The size of the city is given as 12,000 furlongs, which would be approximately 1500 miles in our measuring system. It is not clear if this means a total circumference (4 X 475 miles = 1500 miles), or if the length of each side is 1500 miles. Whichever it is, be assured that it will be a massive city with plenty of room for all.

6. **What marks off the perimeters of the city?**

> *"Also she had a great and high wall with twelve gates, and twelve angels at the gates, and names written on them, which are the names of the twelve tribes of the children of Israel: three gates on the east, three gates on the north, three gates on the south, and three gates on the west. Now the wall of the city had twelve foundations, and on them were the names of the twelve apostles of the Lamb." Revelation 21:12-14.*

The entire city is surrounded by **A GREAT AND HIGH WALL**. The enormous and impressive wall system is not to keep people out, but to control traffic in and out of the city. There is an elaborate gate system with twelve gates evenly distributed around the city, allowing for a controlled flow of traffic from every direction of the compass. Apparently, there will be a no-fly zone established over the city area.

7. **What is the main attraction in this city?**

> *"And there shall be no more curse, but the throne of God and of the Lamb shall be in it, and His servants shall serve Him." Revelation 22:3.*

THE THRONE OF GOD being inside this city has far-reaching significance. The city is the new headquarters for God's universe. Those passing through the gates will not be local residents, but mostly foreign visitors from all over God's universe, on their way to the throne of God. The last leg of their journey to God's throne will take them down our streets. We will have opportunity to greet and talk with them, perhaps even inviting them home with us after they have finished their business at God's throne.

8. **What are the main building materials used?**

> *"The construction of its wall was of jasper; and the city was pure gold, like clear glass." Revelation 21:18.*

JASPER AND PURE GOLD are both described as clear (probably translucent), allowing light to pass through them. See verse 11. The light passing through such precious materials will add hues and shades to the glorious light from God that will please and excite the senses of all. It will be a deeply stirring experience to walk through such a glory-enhanced light. Common stone is opaque, blocking any light that falls on it, but all precious stones are translucent, adding character to the light that passes through it.

9. **What is written on the gates of the city?**

   "Also she had a great and high wall with twelve gates, and twelve angels at the gates, and names written on them, which are the names of the twelve tribes of the children of Israel: three gates on the east, three gates on the north, three gates on the south, and three gates on the west." Revelation 21:12, 13.

Each gate has a name, indicating it opened to a certain section of the city. The gates are assigned **THE NAMES OF THE TWELVE TRIBES OF ISRAEL.**

In all ancient, walled cities of the Bible, the gates were more than mere openings in the town's wall. The area immediately inside each gate was elaborate, similar to our "town squares" today. They served as a center for community activities, such as business transactions; legal matters; group meetings; and public markets. In the New Jerusalem each gate will be assigned to a particular tribe. Evidently, all the residents will be registered under one or another of these divisions, and will seek out the gate area of his assigned tribe for community affairs and matters of general interest.

The New Earth

The last chapters of Revelation are so taken up with describing this most impressive city from God that the account never returns to give details about the rest of the new creation that will appear. However, we are not totally deprived of any information about that new environment and life which planet earth will enjoy. There are several pictures of life in that new earth given in previous Scripture that will fill in the details for us.

10. **What special thing will God do?**

    "Then He who sat on the throne said, Behold, I make all things new. And He said to me, Write, for these words are true and faithful." Revelation 21:5.

This is a very special announcement that comes with God's strong affirmation as being "true and faithful." He intends to **MAKE ALL THINGS NEW**.

The fires of hell have destroyed everyone and everything impacted by sin in this world. In order for this planet to be once again fit for human habitation, God must do all over again what He did on those original six days of creation. In the Genesis creation, man did not witness the process, for he was created at the end of the week. In this creation spoken of in Revelation, human beings will be able to be eyewitnesses from the walls of the New Jerusalem.

11. What kind of bodies will we already have?

> *"For our citizenship is in heaven, from which we also eagerly wait for the Savior, the Lord Jesus Christ, who will transform our lowly body that it may be conformed to His glorious body, according to the working by which He is able even to subdue all things to Himself."* Philippians 3:20, 21.

The first new thing God will do for us is to give us **BODIES LIKE CHRIST'S GLORIOUS BODY.** At the resurrection and rapture we will experience a body change (see I Corinthians 15:51-54), so there is nothing more God needs to do for us so that we can enjoy eternity. Because we will be in bodily form, as we are now, God must make the things of this world new again for our use and enjoyment.

12. What two tasks will occupy some of our time?

> *"They shall build houses and inhabit them; they shall plant vineyards and eat their fruit. They shall not build and another inhabit; they shall not plant and another eat; for as the days of a tree, so shall be the days of My people, and My elect shall long enjoy the work of their hands."* Isaiah 65:21, 22.

We will **BUILD HOUSES** and **PLANT VINEYARDS** (gardens for food), just as we do now. Our homes in the heavenly city have been pre-built for us by Jesus, but once the earth has been recreated we will be able to go out and choose a lovely location where we can build a country home for ourselves. We will also produce our own food (vineyards). No one will sell food, or any commodity. This means we will have a cashless society. What a drastic social change that will create among mankind!

13. **What will never happen to man or animal?**

　　"The wolf and the lamb shall feed together; the lion shall eat straw like the ox, and dust shall be the serpent's food. They shall not hurt nor destroy in all My holy mountain, says the Lord." Isaiah 65:25.

No man and no animal will **HURT OR BE DESTROYED**. Animals will lose their ferociousness and once again become the beloved companions of man. Man will be safe around these animals. Also, the animals will be safe around man. The animal kingdom, as well as human beings, will be vegetarians.

14. **What two events will be observed by all?**

　　"For as the new heavens and the new earth which I will make shall remain before Me, says the Lord, so shall your descendants and your name remain. And it shall come to pass that from one New Moon to another, and from one Sabbath to another, all flesh shall come to worship Me, says the Lord." Isaiah 66:22, 23.

Believers in Bible times were very familiar with **NEW MOONS** and **WEEKLY SABBATHS**. In the Old Testament, the New Moon festival was not a holy day, but a time of festive gathering. According to Revelation 22:2, the tree of life will play a prominent role in this monthly celebration. The Sabbath day will continue to be the weekly, holy day God originally made it. Its blessings will be enjoyed by the redeemed for all eternity.

It is within the realm of possibility for each one of us to be there to enjoy that new life, new earth, and new city. "It is your Father's good pleasure to give you the kingdom," Jesus said in Luke 12:32. To help us get ready, He stands behind that statement with the assurance of His grace. If you accept Christ into your life just now and follow His commandments in full surrender, "Your reward will be great." Luke 6:35.

QUIZ FOR LESSON NO. 21
List five new things we will enjoy in eternity.

1. _____

_____

2. _____

_____

3. _____

_____

4. _____

_____

5. _____

_____

QUIZ ANSWERS

LESSON NO. 2
1. False
2. True
3. True
4. False
5. False

LESSON NO. 3
1. White
2. Red
3. Black
4. Pale
5. White

LESSON NO. 4
1. B
2. B
3. C
4. A
5. B

LESSON NO. 5
1. No
2. No
3. Yes
4. No
5. No

LESSON NO. 6
1. B
2. D
3. E
4. C
5. A

LESSON NO 7
1. C
2. A
3. C
4. B
5. C

LESSON NO 8
1. False
2. False
3. True
4. True
5. True

LESSON NO. 9
1. A or C
2. B
3. C
4. B or C
5. A

LESSON NO 10
1. Scales
2. Sabbath
3. Seventh
4. Sign
5. Special

LESSON NO. 11
Church Attendance
Bible Study
Walk in Nature
Rest
Enjoy Sacred Music

QUIZ ANSWERS

LESSON NO. 12
1. DECEPTION
2. BIBLE
3. TRUTH
4. PERISH
5. HEART

LESSON NO. 13
1. C
2. A
3. B
4. C
5. C

LESSON NO. 14
1. A
2. B
3. C
4. C or A
5. C

LESSON NO. 15
1. True
2. True
3. True
4. False
5. False

LESSON NO. 16
Great Earthquake
Sun Becomes Black
Moon Becomes Like Blood
Stars Fall
Heavens Split Open as a Scroll
Wonders in Heavens & Earth
Mountains & Islands Move

LESSON NO. 17
1. B
2. B
3. B
4. B
5. B

LESSON NO. 18
1. B
2. C
3. A
4. B
5. B or C

LESSON NO. 19
1. A or B
2. B
3. C
4. C
5. A

LESSON NO. 20
1. False
2. False
3. False
4. True
5. True

LESSON NO. 21
New City
New Earth
New Body
New House
New Animals
New Light
New Water

NOTES

NOTES